Privatization and Deregulation in the Gulf Energy Sector

PRIVATIZATION AND DEREGULATION IN THE GULF ENERGY SECTOR

THE EMIRATES CENTER FOR STRATEGIC
STUDIES AND RESEARCH

The Emirates Center for Strategic Studies and Research

The Emirates Center for Strategic Studies and Research (ECSSR) is an independent research institution dedicated to the promotion of professional studies and educational excellence in the UAE, the Gulf, and the Arab world. Since its establishment in Abu Dhabi in 1994, ECSSR has served as a focal point for scholarship on political, economic, and social matters. Indeed, ECSSR is at the forefront of analysis and commentary on Arab affairs.

The Center seeks to provide a forum for the scholarly exchange of ideas by hosting conferences and symposia, organizing workshops, sponsoring a lecture series, and publishing original and translated books and research papers. ECSSR also has an active fellowship and grant program for the writing of scholarly books and for the translation, into Arabic, of works relevant to the Center's mission. Moreover, ECSSR has a large library including rare and specialized holdings, and a state-of-the-art technology center, which has developed an award-winning website that is a unique and comprehensive source of information on the Gulf.

Through these and other activities, ECSSR aspires to engage in mutually beneficial professional endeavors with comparable institutions worldwide, and to contribute to the general educational and scientific development of the UAE.

Published in 1999 by
The Emirates Center for Strategic Studies and Research
PO Box 4567, Abu Dhabi, United Arab Emirates
website: http://www.ecssr.ac.ae

Distributed by British Academic Press
Victoria House, Bloomsbury Square, London WC1B 4DZ
175 Fifth Avenue, New York, NY 10010

A full CIP record of this book is available from the British Library
A full CIP record of this book is available from the US Library of Congress

Library of Congress catalog card number: available

ISBN 1 86064 410 4 hardback
ISBN 1 86064 411 2 paperback

Contents

Figures and Tables

Figures

Tables

Abbreviations and Acronyms

ADNOC	Abu Dhabi National Oil Company
ALBA	Aluminium Bahrain B.S.C.
APM	administered pricing mechanism
ARAMCO	Arabian American Oil Company
ASRY	Arab Shipbuilding and Repair Yard
BATELCO	Bahrain Telecommunications Company
bbl	barrels
bbbl	billion barrels
BDB	Bahrain Development Bank
bmt	billion metric tonnes
BNOC	British National Oil Company
BOO	Build-Own-Operate
BOOT	Build-Own-Operate-Transfer
BOT	Build-Own-Transfer
BP	British Petroleum
CEGB	Central Electricity Generating Board
ECA	Economic Cooperation Act
ESI	electricity supply industry
FOB	free on board
GCC	Gulf Co-operation Council
GDP	gross domestic product
GOI	Government of India
GPIC	Gulf Petrochemical Industries Company
HSD	high speed diesel
IPO	initial public offering
IPP	Independent Power Projects (in MacKerron: Independent Power Plants)
IWPP	Independent Water and Power Projects
kgoe	kilogram of oil equivalent
KIA	Kuwait Investment Authority
KOC	Kuwait Oil Company
KPC	Kuwait Petroleum Company
kW	kilowatt
LC	local currency

LLC	limited liability company
LNG	liquefied natural gas
LPG	liquefied petroleum gas
LRF	Limited Recourse Financing
MoPNG	Ministry of Petroleum and Natural Gas
MS	mild steel
mtoe	million tonnes of oil equivalent
MW	megawatts
NGC	National Grid Company
O&M	operating and maintenance
OECD	Organisation for Economic Co-operation and Development
OFFER	Office of Electricity Regulation
OPEC	Organization of Petroleum Exporting Companies
PDO	Petroleum Development Oman
PdVSA	Petróleos de Venezuela Sociedad Anonima
PE	private enterprise
PPA	Power Purchase Agreement
QATARGAS	Qatar Liquefied Gas Company
QPC	Qatar Petroleum Company
R&D	research and development
SCECO	Saudi Consolidated Electricity Company
tcm	trillion cubic meters
TERI	Tata Energy Research Institute
UAE	United Arab Emirates
UK	United Kingdom
US	United States of America
WED	Water and Electricity Department
YPF	Yacimientos Petroliferos Fiscales

Privatizing Energy: An Overview

Michael Kuczynski

An Idea Whose Time Has Come

State holdings in raw material production, in infrastructure, and in basic industries were standard – worldwide – among the institutional responses to the strains of the Great Depression and World War II. In developing countries, some time between the 1930s and the 1950s, these holdings became part of the undisputed institutional baggage of the pattern of development known as "import substitution." State enterprises went hand-in-hand with regulated bank-based finance, restrictions on foreign investment, institutionalized social security, and public employment programs, as well as with a certain amount of industrial protectionism. They were accepted as instrumental for both efficiency and equity in resource allocation, and viewed as essential equipment in dealing with market failures. Indeed, state enterprises continued to be part of institutional orthodoxy well after import substitution itself had passed its own doctrinal expiration date.[1]

After a vogue of 50 years, the idea that state holdings are indispensable in some activities is now once again defunct. Why? It is tempting to attribute the change to greater consciousness of potential efficiency gains – maybe also potential equity gains – through improved structures of ownership, competition, and governance. These are effects of the sort analyzed in this volume. But before considering this aspect, it should also be recognized that a more general tendency has been at work to promote the move away from state holdings, whatever its specific merits in individual economic activities.

The international settlement which ushered in the urge to decentralize, privatize, and readjust local regulatory regimes – in the overall process

1

known as "globalization" – has occurred, as most fundamental changes do, in a rather piecemeal fashion. There were early converts (as far apart as Britain and Chile) as well as remarkably reluctant followers (as diverse as Brazil and Germany). All the same, the process has displayed a central inexorable logic of its own, associated with a number of key international institutional changes at the turn of the 1990s.

At the core of the process is the Uruguay Round of the General Agreement on Tariffs and Trade (GATT) together with its corollaries in the area of international finance. The Uruguay Round itself resulted in a two-way bargain whereby producers of raw materials and manufacturers are to get better access to export markets on the understanding that hitherto "sheltered" sectors – typically financial services, media, transportation, communications, and utilities – are opened up to foreign investment. Although quite general in application, the bargain bears directly on the relationship between the Organisation for Economic Co-operation and Development (OECD) countries and the developing world. In effect, the latter get improved access to markets for their production in "tradeables" as the *quid pro quo* for opening up their production in "non-tradeables" to investment by the former. This basic exchange is coupled with the adoption of more flexible, market-based approaches to capital importing and foreign debt management than had characterized earlier arrangements.[2]

The settlement makes sense in a number of ways. It can be claimed, for instance, that if the problem of surges in capital flows is overlooked, what is known as the "transfer problem" stands a better chance of being resolved; those importing capital are provided with a more secure outlet for the exports they need to make in order to service their external exposures. More generally, the settlement represents a potential improvement in the mechanism which allocates savings to investment internationally. Under the arrangements prevailing until the 1990s, the net worth of activities in sheltered sectors was probably significantly reduced by insulation from pressure to rationalize technological or managerial choices. Nor is it obvious that the gains from the settlement are asymmetrically distributed against those opening up to foreign investment. Indeed, it is possible that they may gain at the expense of those opening up to trade.[3]

It follows that the dismantling of state holdings, for example in energy, is not just a local response to potential efficiency gains – even though it may seem so at the level of individual activities. It is a component in an extensive redefinition of international economic order. The widespread readjustment of micro-regulatory regimes, involving decentralization, deregulation, and privatization, observed in advanced and developing countries alike, is not only a by-product of a wide ranging settlement in the world economy; it is also driven by that settlement. Where the merits of state versus private holding are closely balanced, the new international economic order calls for the private or mixed mode. As such, it represents a tendency not easily resisted; full assessment of its benefits and costs involves broader issues in international political economy than the more technical ones to which we now turn.

Privatization in Itself

Abstracting from its international context, the idea of privatization is mainly concerned with two issues: effectiveness of incentives and distribution of gains or losses.[4] Incentives are intended to make economic activity in a particular sector compatible with public welfare. The incentives at issue in privatization arise from the way in which ownership is restructured – replacing a holding whose income streams accrue to the state with a holding whose income streams accrue to "stakeholders" in the capital market in accordance with the structure of corporate finance adopted in the privatization or determined by subsequent adjustments. The problem of distribution arises if, as is likely, the restructuring of ownership involves some changes in relative net worth among the parties to the transaction.

In a wonderland world of frictionless access to information, costless transactions, and perfect insurance, the issue of how the ownership of enterprises should be structured is a matter of near-complete indifference.[5] For instance, if taxation is neutral and there is no difference between the financial constraints or time horizons imposed by the general public on economic activity through government or through the capital market, a state enterprise whose funds flow through the public sector budget is indistinguishable in its effects on general welfare from a quoted company which has issued claims on the capital market. If there were any difference, competition would see to its elimination. Transfer between one structure of ownership and the other would be a toss up; the present value of all future expected net worth effects on taxpayers of the public enterprise structure would be identical to that of the quoted-company structure. This would be so even if (as may be the case significantly in primary energy) reassignments of economic "rents" were involved.[6]

In the real world, however, imperfections in information, taxation, opportunism, and competition are such that the structure of ownership is a matter of great importance. It affects incentives and the distribution of gains and losses across the population, and these determine quite a lot of what the general public gets out of economic activity. The earlier justifications of state enterprises were various:

- Benefits in the form of stability of output and avoidance of wasteful competition;
- Adequacy of horizons for investment planning;
- The possibility of an integrated sectoral, as opposed to narrowly corporate, view of investment needs;
- Appropriate pricing of outputs and inputs, and accommodation of disadvantaged customers;
- Responsiveness to regional needs and to public opinion; and
- Protection of national interests.

Implied in the earlier vision was a stark choice between an integrated state enterprise whose operations and overall impact on the economy are benevolently controlled by alert ministers and a monopolistic private enterprise helplessly watched by a regulatory body which has been "captured" by the industry.

In practice, however, the running of state enterprises – while it may at times have delivered some of these benefits – has often involved administrative slack, a drain on public finances, and unwarranted promotion of sectional interests. For a variety of reasons, ministers and government departments have been unable, or perhaps unwilling, to structure incentives adequately or to identify negative effects on the general public.[7] Where state enterprises have performed well, it is generally because of a structure of incentives which makes them functionally indistinguishable from private enterprises. Moreover, it has become obvious that the integrated character of many state holdings need not carry over into the privatized state, so that the introduction of competition into an activity being privatized can be used to offset potential regulatory weakness.

It is true that, unless the time horizon is very long, reform of existing arrangements is not the same as starting from scratch. The fact that an alternative mode of ownership, if introduced from the start, might have been superior to the one currently in use does not necessarily warrant change. The present value of the costs of change must be assessed against prospective gains from change. The capital market will need to be given some incentive to buy out part or all of the state's interest – an incentive such as some undervaluation of assets, some untapped rationalization or borrowing potential, some tax advantage.[8] At the same time, part of the state's debt can be transferred into the capital structure of the privatized entity. Moreover, various components of the existing capital stock (including skills) may be left "stranded" by the change, although this is less of a problem where – as in the Gulf and in developing countries generally – energy consumption is rising rapidly.[9]

So the state as seller needs to check that after transactions costs, and taking into account effective "gearing" (i.e., "leverage") and stranded costs, the present value of the net tax revenue to be expected from the profits of the privatized operation, plus the proceeds of the privatization sale, do not fall short of the windfall granted to the capital market. If there were a shortfall, it would be a matter of knowing whether or not other gains exceed other losses, suitably weighted by the importance attached to the various recipients. Because the state does, after all, repeatedly redistribute net worth through all sorts of routine tax or regulatory changes, the fact that there may be losses or losers is not necessarily an impediment to change. Nonetheless, these considerations do underline the importance of ensuring that tax systems and structures of corporate ownership are consistent in their aims.

Privatization in Relation to the Energy Sector

In energy there are two basic stages of production, each with its further by-products: upstream involves securing access to primary resources as inputs (oil, gas, or other); downstream transforms these into secondary energy output (electricity, heat, or other by-products). At either stage, there may be economic rents involved. The downstream rents are likely to be relatively uniform and, if competition is at all present, they are likely to be low. They are, after all, returns to technological know-how or to management skills, both of which are quite widely available – particularly if the time frame under consideration is long enough. This is not so in upstream; in primary production, the rents are returns to quality (for instance quality of extractive deposits), so that they are not necessarily uniform and do not disappear through competition. A low cost or high quality deposit remains so until it is exhausted or recovery technology is modified.

The upshot of this distinction is that the reasons for restructuring ownership may well differ. For downstream production, it is more straightforwardly a matter of efficiency, in the sense that what is at issue is aggregate net-worth enhancement (win-win), rather than a significant reshuffling of rents, at least if the problem of stranded capacity is over-looked. For upstream production, in primary energy, while net-worth enhancement is most probably also involved, reassignment of rents may be more significantly present, and so there may be an element of net-worth transfer (win-lose).

Consider the case of private ownership in the primary sector. It is, of course, appropriate that private claims to economic rents be taxed. Indeed, it is inconceivable that they should not be taxed, for economic rents are close to ideal as a base for taxation; the rent is created by the allocation of the property concession, the incidence of the tax is clear, it cannot be shaken, and modification of economic behavior to avoid taxation is pointless. Moreover, under private ownership, taxation can be a key instrument in achieving an appropriate rate of resource depletion.[10] These considerations are all the more pertinent in the case of national resource rents vis-à-vis foreign investors. All the same, there is a difficulty. Since in principle the effective tax rate on rents can go to 100 percent without possibility of escape, and this is a threat clear to potential investors, it is only in special cases that a stable rate of taxation – and hence a stable interest in ownership – can be achieved. In effect, what is required is a framework of long run political trust between the parties concerned. If the tax rate seems low, investors can rationally foreshadow a rise and the value of the asset drops unless hasty depletion is possible, or a "race to the bottom" can confidently be expected among states in terms of tax rates. If the tax rate seems high, there may be no point in investing. Were the resource price (e.g., the oil price) stable in real terms – its level determines the economic rent – an arrangement which remains mutually satisfactory to the private investor and to the general public or the state might be achieved. But in practice, the real price of extractive resources displays long swings as well as short run fluctuations.

So, although private capital in the ownership of deposits (as opposed to exploration and exploitation) is still commonplace in primary energy, there is a genuine difficulty all the same, and privatization of basic ownership poses distinct problems. This does not, of course, preclude efficient injection of private capital (through joint ventures, BOOT [build-own-operate-transfer] and other schemes) at various stages of primary production close ownership of the deposits themselves.[11] The efficiencies of such participation are akin to those to be found downstream.

Privatization of Utilities

Utilities are activities which face generally predictable demand for their output, and involve lumpy investments with long payback periods and generally predictable depreciation. The combination of demand and payback or depreciation characteristics on the one hand, and lumpiness on the other, generates a standard quandary. Cash-flows are predictable, which means that the lumpiness can easily be handled by standard financial mechanisms and there is no serious obstacle to structuring the ownership through the capital market (i.e., through bond and equity issues). In effect, it is easy to securitize utilities. But at the same time, lumpiness raises the possibility of a situation of monopoly, while some of the characteristics of demand and depreciation imply that in such a situation a monopolist answerable to capital market incentives might engage in undesirable practices, such as market rigging through cross-subsidization between different categories of customers. This suggests, or at any rate used to suggest, the need for some form of regulation. Alternatively, ownership should not be structured through the capital market but through some form of state holding.

As has already been noted, from the 1930s to the 1980s, the general tendency – with rare exceptions outside the United States, all of them considered to be quite remarkable – was to resolve the quandary through the state. Since the late 1980s, the tendency has been the other way, i.e., to consider ownership through the capital market not only as an idea whose time has come, but as the norm; the state holding idea has become passé. The reason for this change is twofold. There is the general institutional mood of the globalized economy; and besides, at the level of the activities themselves (i.e., in utilities), the balance of probabilities has shifted from a position where monopoly was thought inevitable and regulation likely to be defective, while ministerial control over public enterprises could only be beneficial. The new view is that even if regulation has its defects, monopolistic outcomes are not inevitable and ministerial control of public enterprises is likely to be an unsatisfactory way of absorbing pressures on the public purse. This is largely a development which results from learning about manning and pricing in the industries in question.

The Introduction of Market Mechanisms

In general terms, the object of privatization and of its associated mechanisms of competition is to install a structure of ownership and control – including decentralization – the performance of which, in relation to the general public's welfare, is to be evaluated in terms of a dual price and quality criterion. One, does the schedule of charges minimize cost to the consumer while ensuring that, on the one hand, operational costs are covered and, on the other, an appropriate cost of capital is met?[12] And, two, is investment, and hence the resulting quality of supply of services, appropriate? These are obviously interrelated requirements, and the three main steps in the process of privatization – setting up the commercial structure of the industry, deciding on the regulatory framework, and selling off the industry – are instrumental in determining whether or not the object is achieved.

There are, of course, choices at each step:
- How far to unbundle the industry, i.e., whether to treat transmission as the only component sacrosanct enough to be left whole, and decentralize everything else, or to be swayed by the merits of vertical or horizontal integration (e.g., to reduce exposure to risk);
- How to reconcile regulation of price or profitability with adequacy of investment; and
- How widely to disperse the ownership, through what sort of financial intermediaries, and with how much "gearing."

If the industry is extensively decentralized, the resulting competition will do much to mitigate the well-known problems associated with excessive reliance on regulation; also the BOOT structure chosen to link up the industry with the operator affects the cost of debt and therefore the cost of capital. If regulation is done with adequate understanding of the industry's operational problems, imperfections in the (vertical or horizontal) commercial structure of the industry become less important. If privatizing is done with adequately high indebtedness, "bonding" is likely to enhance managerial sensitivity to the market.[13] An adequate balance must be struck, and there are a multiplicity of combinations that work – though the dual lesson of most privatizations in the downstream energy sector appears to be that it is best not to rely overmuch on perfection, either in the regulatory process[14] or in the operation of the capital market.[15] Greater reliance on competition, which is the remedy, does however keep bumping up against a key difficulty: how to charge different supplier-consumer pairings for use of the element of natural monopoly in the industry, the transmission network.[16]

Appropriate supply involves meeting growth in (time varying) demand from different categories of customer, retail and wholesale – a problem which typically involves deploying a range of different capacities in generation.[17] In a system of decentralized supply, the system of charges which results from the combination of regulation and competition must be such as to remunerate those different capacities adequately. It is in this context that, in mature utility systems in particular, the problem of "stranded" capacities arises.[18] Likewise, decentralization of ownership or control needs to be structured so as to be consistent with appropriate incentives, in particular as regards risks. These broadly divide into the operational, the political or regulatory, and the exogenous. Operational risks are internal to the utility itself, i.e., they arise from construction or operation, and so far as possible should be reflected to the operator by the way in which the commercial structure of the industry has been set – in other words how it is unbundled and corporatized, and what the nature of the contracts is between the component parts. (If operational risks are not reflected to the operator, there is moral hazard.) Political risks arise through the regulatory and tax relationship which remains between the utility and the state after privatization. These risks are most appropriately controlled by adopting, as a point of civics, the idea that infrastructure which is intended to serve more than one generation should be planned in accordance with intergenerational time horizons; if the private supplier shows willingness to do so, then the regulatory and tax system should take the pledge not to be fickle. Exogenous risks are generally macro-economic, pertaining in practice mainly to the price of primary energy and foreign exchange. Private operators can and should hedge these through normal market mechanisms.

Ultimately the object of privatizing utilities should be to achieve transparency and accountability in the running of essential infrastructure, right down to mundane details such as stopping leakage and waste, and ensuring payment of bills. It is by focusing on practical objectives in the restructuring of ownership that the public interest is best served. As far as the net worth of the state is concerned, the real fiscal effects lie not in immediate proceeds to the budget from asset sales, but in the present value of all future revenue (and diminished subsidy) effects associated with improved operation of these activities under a different structure of ownership and an appropriate tax regime. In an international context, the advantage of privatization, in terms of conforming to the new international economic order, is most probably an added bonus.

This Volume

In terms of management of the energy sector, the Gulf states are of interest for four distinct reasons. The first is the dominance – for many decades to come – of the primary energy sector as a component of economic activity in those countries, both on the side of demand for national output, including services, and on the side of supply as a key source of national income, involving substantial fluctuation in the terms of trade. The second is the region's relatively high, though fluctuating, per capita demand for secondary energy, which derives from the region's level of income. The third reason in terms of distinctive interest lies in the region's still relatively low use of gas-fueled generation. The fourth lies in the fact that the regional cooperation which already exists in the primary sector can be extended to the secondary, though as yet this has not much been the case. As experience in Europe and North America shows, when it comes to matching given capacities to variable load demand, there are distinct advantages in the versatility of small scale gas-fueled generation and in cross-border exchanges of surpluses. Among contiguous countries with relatively small populations and relatively high levels of per capita income, integration of markets for utilities may, in practical terms, be as rewarding a form of regional cooperation as other more ambitious forms of integration.[19]

This volume contains contributions to the analysis of privatization in the energy sector from three different perspectives. From the standpoint of the Gulf states, the concern is mainly with operations in the downstream sector for the simple reason that in countries where the economic rent from primary production looms large in national income, privatization upstream is implausible other than in ancillary activities. Sharif Ghalib opens the discussion by reviewing the scope for privatization both in terms of the role of the energy industry in the Gulf states and of the state of the capital markets there. Hafeez Shaikh then examines the progress of privatization in the region overall, particularly in secondary energy, highlighting obstacles to progress and technical points to be addressed. Andrew Ward considers the requisite legal framework into which – in the

Emirates – the restructuring of ownership would be and is being fitted, drawing attention to the constraints imposed on the process by the lack of an overall legal instrument for privatization.

The second part of the volume is concerned with the experience and commercialization of operations in energy production outside the Gulf and mainly upstream in primary production. This perspective is relevant to the Gulf states in terms of general lessons, although Leena Srivastava and Rajnish Goswani also draw out implications for investment plans by Gulf producers. They discuss recent developments in India's oil and gas sector. In particular, they consider the challenges that it poses for participation by foreign capital. Then Paul Horsnell reviews British experience in disposing of state holdings in primary energy, contrasting the cases of oil and gas, and also the very different pioneering experience of the utilities sector. The chapter is pessimistic about privatization upstream, as regards both the problem of economic rent, and the practicalities of flotation on local capital markets.

The third part of the volume deals with experience and lessons downstream in the industry. Gordon MacKerron provides an account of the privatization of electricity in England and Wales since the mid-1980s, stressing that – for all its eventual successes – such a process is bound to involve teething problems, so that it takes time for the net benefits to show through in the industry's new steady-state. This may be an argument for gradualism instead of rapid restructuring. Colin Robinson then supplies an overview of privatization experience and know-how, dealing with the broader political context and, in particular, with the role which competition has to play (in all but the natural monopoly of transmission) in offsetting the weaknesses of regulation. In the concluding chapter, Ibrahim Elwan, Achilles Adamantiades, and Khalid Shadid, stressing the role that deregulation and privatization have to play mainly downstream, identify a ledger of net benefits to be obtained from decentralizing and restructuring ownership in the energy sector of the Gulf states. They conclude, along with the other contributors to this volume, that deregulation and privatization are indeed, for this key regional industry, an idea whose time has come.

I join the authors in thanking Dave Pender, Herro Mustafa, and Susan Al-Baker of ECSSR for their not insignificant contribution to the editing of this volume.

CHAPTER 1

The Financial and Capital Market Implications of Privatizing the Energy Sector in the Gulf

Sharif Ghalib

Introduction

This chapter will address the energy sector in a broad sense, i.e., including power and not just the hydrocarbon sectors of the six Gulf Co-operation Council (GCC) states (Bahrain, Kuwait, Oman, Qatar, Saudi Arabia, and the United Arab Emirates). The issue of capital market development in the GCC is critical for the future growth of this region in light of the following two phenomena:

- An outlook for oil that is not sanguine for the next several years; and
- Key trends in the global economy.

Both pose increasing challenges for the GCC governments and private sectors, both financial and non-financial, if stated long-term objectives for the GCC economies are to be met successfully. Four main points will be addressed in the following sections: future expenditure, dependence on hydrocarbons, challenges and global competition for capital, and alternative sources of revenue and financing.

Future Expenditure

Governments of the six GCC states are contemplating the expenditure of tens of billions of dollars over the next five to ten years, not only on petroleum – both upstream development and downstream expansion – and huge gas projects, but also very sizeable projects in their power sectors.

For GCC states, it has been estimated that expenditure on oil and gas could well be US$100 billion until the year 2010, including US$20 billion on oil refining alone over the next ten years. Estimates suggest that expenditure on major energy projects over the next three to five years will be nearly US$80 billion, including US$34 billion for oil and gas, US$18 billion for petrochemicals, and at least US$13 billion for power.[1] Over the next ten years, including the GCC gas and power grids – if they materialize – GCC outlays on oil, gas, and power alone could be between US$90 and US$100 billion.

Dependence on Hydrocarbons

The GCC account for nearly 49 percent of the world's proved oil reserves and almost 15 percent of proved gas reserves. Despite success in diversifying the economic base, revenue from hydrocarbons still accounts for 90 percent or more of merchandise exports and more than 75 percent of budget revenues. The problem this heavy dependency poses is that the outlook for oil prices is not sanguine for the next several years, given strong and sustained competition from non-OPEC sources of supply which is likely to constrain the demand for GCC oil output over at least the medium-term.

Oil prices were stronger than expected between 1995 and 1997. Indeed, the price of Brent through September of 1997 averaged approximately US$19.3/bbl (see Appendix Table 1.1). While lower than its 1996 average price of US$20.60/bbl, many oil price pundits had been forecasting between US$16.00/bbl and US$18.00/bbl for this period.

The higher than expected price during this period reflects three main factors: continued growth in demand for oil, particularly from Asian countries; slower than projected expansion in non-OPEC production; and low commercial inventories of oil due partly to the relatively recent adoption of just-in-time inventory management by the global petroleum industry.

Larger than anticipated government revenue from oil, stronger private sector activity, the strength of the dollar – to which all regional currencies are tied, resulting in an improvement in GCC terms of trade – combined with continued expansion of non-hydrocarbon exports, including petrochemical volumes, resulted in a substantial improvement in the GCC aggregate current account, which swung into a surplus of US$8.3 billion in 1996 for the first time in several years (see Table 1.1).

Table 1.1

GCC Current Account Balances (US$ million)

Country	1992	1993	1994	1995	1996
Saudi Arabia	17,740	17,268	10,487	5,324	215
UAE	3,686	948	455	400[1]	1,900[1]
Kuwait	450	1,938	2,489	4,574	6,773
Oman	592	1,191	984	801	265
Qatar	9	497	900	700[1]	300[1]
Bahrain	754	35	198	557	0
GCC Total	23,231	21,877	15,513	12,356	9,453

Note
1 Provisional estimates.

Source: IMF, IFS, Official Statistics; GIC, Economics Division Estimates.

It is important to note, however, that spot crude oil prices have been in decline. Indeed, since March 1998, amid mounting physical evidence of an oversupplied global crude market, benchmark crude prices have dipped to their lowest level in almost a decade, with West Texas Intermediate falling to US$13.32/bbl, Brent to US$11.32/bbl, and Dubai to US$9.98/bbl.

Challenges

GCC governments cannot count on a substantial increase in oil revenue during that time frame to fully finance their planned economic and social development projects. The challenge is made more intense by the fact that many other emerging markets are freeing up their economies quickly and also need large volumes of funds to finance their projects. As a result, global competition for capital – including loanable funds but particularly direct investment, both equity and portfolio – is mounting intensely.

Alternative Sources of Revenue and Financing

Alternative sources of revenue and financing must be found that will include two elements. The first element, according to the private sector – both local and foreign – is a larger role in domestic economies through faster development of local money and capital markets and provision of stronger incentives to the foreign investor. This would help fulfill a key stated objective of GCC governments, which is to reduce their role as engines of growth in favor of a larger and ever-growing role in the development process. Furthermore, the hope is that this can be achieved without substantial, additional external borrowing and further depletion of foreign assets. These objectives could, obviously, be partially met by fostering the growth of domestic capital markets which could allow:

- Domestic borrowers, including parastatals, to tap domestic liquidity, which is substantial;
- The opening of local investment opportunities for the private sector, both GCC and expatriate, thereby contributing to reducing capital outflow;
- The repatriation of funds invested abroad; and
- The development of equity and bond markets to facilitate privatization and to stimulate the inflow of foreign investment.

As for the second element, there has been and will continue to be growing recourse to external funding, including commercial bank and Economic Cooperation Act (ECA) guaranteed borrowing, project finance and private financing mechanisms, and substantial borrowing through international bond issuance.

In other words, to fund the costs of huge projects in the energy sector over the next decade, GCC states are likely to tap not only one source of finance but utilize a broad range of internal and external funding mechanisms.

GCC Capital Markets

GCC stock markets have witnessed substantial growth and a noticeable increase in activity recently, particularly over the past two years. These trends are reflected in the data presented in Table 1.2 and Appendix Table 1.5.

The expansion of these stock markets reflects two key developments that are irreversible. The first is encouragement by GCC governments of greater participation in domestic economies by the private sector, especially local but increasingly also the foreign private sector. The second development is the move towards so-called privatization of domestic economies. Much of the privatization that has taken place so far in the GCC has merely been the total or partial sale of state-owned assets to the

Table 1.2

GCC Stock Markets

Market Capitalization (US$ billion and Price Indices, % Change)

Mid–September 1997

Country	Index	% Increase from 31 December 1996	Market Capitalization
Saudi Arabia (NCFEI)	186.01	+21.5	55.86
Kuwait (KSE)	2,517.90	+29.6	27.10
UAE (NBAD)	2,783.98	+10.9	16.61
Bahrain (BSE-33)	1,993.39	+26.3	6.48
Oman (MSM)	423.05	104.2	6.27
Qatar (CBQ)	160.77	+25.3	2.67
GCC Total			114.99

Source: *MEED Money*, 26 September 1997.

private sector, or a reallocation of portfolios among government entities. That is, privatization, at least so far and for the most part, has fallen short of putting local economies on a truly private-sector footing, and sub-stantially reducing the role played by bureaucrats in the allocation of economic resources. Privatization by the GCC states has, however, had the dual effect of generating revenue for the state to help cover budget deficits and of stimulating activity in local stock markets.

As shown in Table 1.2, the aggregate market capitalization of GCC stock markets to mid-September 1997 was approximately US$115 billion, modest relative to other regions but up sharply from the end of 1995 (almost US$75 billion) and the end of 1996 (nearly US$90 billion). Average prices had also risen sharply between the end of 1996 and September 1997, ranging from nearly 11 percent in the UAE to over 100 percent in Oman.

In addition to this growth in market capitalization and price indices, there has been a sharp rise in the volume and value of stocks traded. The aggregate annual value of shares traded on GCC stock markets rose from over US$13 billion in 1995 to nearly US$30 billion by the end of 1996. A better measure of trading activity is the turnover ratio (i.e., the annual value of trades normalized by market capitalization) which abstracts from changes in share prices. The rise in turnover ratios in all GCC markets confirms the expansion in real trading activity. This, combined with the increase in market capitalization, indicates that liquidity has improved in the GCC stock markets.

This expansion notwithstanding, GCC capital markets remain relatively limited, although with great future expansion potential. They have not yet become major sources of local financial intermediation relative to banks. Major characteristics of GCC stock markets can be summarized as follows:

- The largest in terms of absolute market capitalization is in Saudi Arabia; the most active is in Kuwait; the largest number of institutions listed are in Oman;
- Turnover in the Saudi market is relatively low because many participants hold on to shares for long periods as if holding pension funds; turnover in the Kuwaiti market is highest partly due to substantial speculation in that market;
- While the number of listed companies has grown in nearly all markets, they fall far short of the total number of companies registered even if not all the latter are eligible for stock market entry;
- Most GCC capital markets (and many companies listed on those markets) require: improvements in the regulatory and supervisory framework, including rules to mitigate insider trading; greater transparency; and the development of a wider array of trading instruments; and
- None have secondary trading mechanisms necessary for rendering markets deeper and more liquid.

Despite these shortcomings, expansion of equity markets within the GCC states has outpaced by far development in local, non-government bond markets. Although GCC states, led by Oman, have begun tapping the international bond market, local bond markets for private sector issues remain virtually non-existent. Most recently, only Bahrain has publicly expressed its desire to begin development of such a market in the context of efforts to stimulate its own equity market and improve its foreign investment regime.

Implications of Privatizing the Energy Sector in the GCC

The movement towards privatizing the economies of the GCC is irreversible. It has been a gradual process but is picking up momentum. In the energy sector, we have already seen at least the partial privatization of retail gas stations in some countries of the GCC.

The second phase of privatization in the energy sector has taken place in the power sectors, led by Oman and the UAE. The Manah Power

Project in Oman was the first to be executed on a private sector financing basis, while Oman and the UAE are implementing other power projects on a build-own-operate (BOO) or BOOT basis. This trend, slow to start, is likely to accelerate. Moreover, the GCC is considering the establishment of a region-wide power grid financed by the private sector, although this project has been held up by a number of problems including the issue of subsidies and, in light of price controls, the issue of government guarantees of tariffs to private sector owners.

Conclusion

Further privatization of the power sector can be expected, coupled with gradual privatization of the downstream hydrocarbon sector, including retail, refining, and petrochemicals, at least secondary and tertiary projects. The real prospect of a gradually expanding role for the private sector in the GCC states – within and outside of the energy sector – will underpin continued expansion of the region's stock markets and, eventually, development of a regional bond market. Movement in that direction is likely to be gradual; it requires improvements in the regulatory and supervisory framework and more effective encouragement of foreign investment. Key constraints to greater foreign investment – which would help foster development of local capital markets – are insistence on local majority ownership and lack of adequate property rights.

These obstacles will be gradually removed over time; indeed, the pace of reform has picked up in the last year or two. The growth of local capital markets is unlikely to be so rapid that it would soon threaten the disintermediation of commercial banks in the region. It is, however, likely to enable the private sector to access the substantial liquidity in this region, reduce pressure on government budgets, and may induce the repatriation of even a small portion of huge assets invested abroad or, at least, slow the outflow of investable funds – held by nationals and expatriates in the GCC – to the international capital market.

Appendix Table 1.1
Spot Oil Prices (US$/bbl) 1991–97

Year	Brent	WTI	OPEC Basket
1991	19.99	21.46	18.62
1992	19.34	20.56	18.44
1993	17.04	18.46	16.33
1994	15.83	17.20	15.53
1995	17.04	18.43	16.88
1996	20.60	22.02	20.20
1997[1]	19.26	20.66	18.98
Jan. 1997	23.54	25.17	23.19
Feb. 1997	20.97	22.21	20.49
Mar. 1997	19.20	21.00	18.64
Q1[2]	21.24	22.79	20.77
Apr. 1997	17.61	19.72	17.46
May 1997	19.00	20.84	18.76
June 1997	17.66	19.17	17.37
Q2	18.09	19.91	17.86
July 1997	18.42	19.63	17.86
Aug. 1997	18.60	19.93	18.08
Sep. 1997	18.30	19.72	17.85
Q3	18.44	19.76	17.93
Oct. 1997	19.10	20.75	19.54
Nov. 1997	19.27	19.97	18.84
Dec. 1997	17.31	18.39	16.89
Q4	18.56	19.70	18.42

Notes

1 Year average through 29 September 1997.

2 Q = quarter.

Sources: For Brent and WTI prices, *Wall Street Journal*, various issues.
For Brent and WTI prices, 1991–94 IMF, IFS, May 1994.
For OPEC Basket, *MEES*, various issues.

Appendix Table 1.2
Average Differentials (US$/bbl) 1991–97

Year	WTI-Brent	Brent-OPEC
1991	1.47	1.37
1992	1.22	0.90
1993	1.42	0.71
1994	1.37	0.30
1995	1.39	0.16
1996	1.42	0.40
1997	1.41	—

Sources: For Brent and WTI prices, *Wall Street Journal*, various issues.
For Brent and WTI prices, 1991–94 IMF, IFS, May 1994.
For OPEC Basket, *MEES*, various issues.

Appendix Figure 1.1
Spot Oil Prices 1991–97

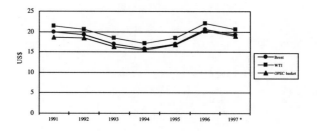

Note
1 refers to year average through 29 September 1997.

Appendix Table 1.3
Stock Markets in the GCC

	Market Capitalization				Trading Value				Price Index	P/E	Rating
	(US$ bn)		(% of GDP)		(US$ bn)		(% of Mkt Cap.)		(%)	(Ratio)	(Moody's)
	1995	1996	1995	1996	1995	1996	1995	1996	1995	1996	1995
S. Arabia	40.9	45.3	32.6	33.3	6.20	6.80	15.2	20.4	+11.7	16.0	Baa3
Kuwait	14.3	21.1	53.8	68.1	6.40	19.20	44.8	91.0	+39.5	17.8	Baa1
UAE[1]	11.5	13.5	28.8	30.3	0.20		1.7		+15.3	13.3	Baa1
Bahrain	4.7	5.0	96.5	99.0	0.10	0.18	2.1	3.6	+16.6	16.5	Ba1
Oman	2.0	2.7	14.5	17.7	0.20	0.70	10.0	25.9	+26.1	17.0	Baa2
Qatar	n/a	2.1	n/a	28.0	n/a	n/a	n/a	n/a	+11.4	n/a	Baa2

Note
1 Unofficial market.

Sources: Federation of Arab Stock Markets, *Arab Stockmarkets*; *MEES*; *MEED Money* and *MEED*; all various
issues. For Rating (of bonds), "Investment Grade = Baa3 and higher."

Appendix Table 1.4
GCC Stock Markets
Public Offers/Placings in GCC

	Bahrain	Kuwait	Oman	UAE	Saudi Arabia	Qatar
Regulations on Public Offers	Yes	Yes	Yes	Yes	Yes	No
Regulations on Private Placings	No	No	No	No	No	No
Public Offer Defined	No	No	No	No	No	No
Private Placing Defined	No	No	No	No	No	No

Sources: "Raising Debt & Equity in the GCC," E.R.J. Cameron, Clifford Chance, paper presented at IIR Conference, 11 May 1997, Dubai, UAE.

Appendix Table 1.5
GCC Stock Markets

	No. of Companies		Cross Listed	Open to Foreign Nationals			
	Listed on Exchange	Registered in Country[2]		GCC[3]	Non-GCC Residents Arab Non-Arab		Non-Resident Foreigners
Saudi Arabia	70	451,621	No	Yes (up to 25%)	Only through SAMBA's Mutual Fund listed on London's Stock Market		
Kuwait	72	110,000	Yes (with Egypt, Lebanon, Bahrain, UAE, and Oman)	Yes	Only through 3 listed Mutual Funds		No
UAE[1]	31	93,267	No	No: Only through the EBI's Equity Fund, initially up to a 20% maximum			
Bahrain	40	29,000	Yes (with Kuwait and Bahrain)	Yes	Restricted to residents of at least 3 years and subject to limits		Limited to 4 listed companies
Oman	111	81,755	Yes (with Kuwait and Bahrain)	Yes	Only through several Mutual Funds subject to a 49% ceiling		
Qatar	18	16,228	No	No	No	No	No

Notes
1 Unofficial market.
2 Refers to 1996 except for Qatar (end-1994).
3 Excluding bank shares.

CHAPTER 2

Privatization of Energy in the Gulf: Selected Issues and Options

Abdul Hafeez Shaikh[1]

Introduction

Most countries in the world are privatizing. Privatization is seen as a pragmatic response to the difficulties of reforming public enterprises, the fiscal constraints facing many governments, and the financing requirements of infrastructure.

Although privatization has come slowly to the Gulf, there are signs that the countries of the region are more interested than ever before in reforming. Some countries have already initiated, and others are about to start, privatization programs that will open areas traditionally under the exclusive domain of the government to the private sector. These programs target infrastructure and public utilities, including those in the important sector of energy. This chapter focuses upon the privatization of energy in the Gulf countries, and will:

- Survey the privatization programs in the Gulf countries, with a focus on energy sector enterprises;
- Explain the reasons for the slow progress of privatization, particularly in the energy sector;
- Make a case for accelerated privatization of energy sector enterprises, particularly those in the power sector; and
- Highlight some issues relevant to the Gulf that will affect the design and implementation of their energy privatizations.

Brief Survey of Privatization Programs

What has been happening on the privatization front in the Gulf countries? In particular, what is the status of energy privatization?

OMAN

Oman was the first Gulf country to initiate an infrastructure privatization program. The government is hoping to raise the national savings rate (via greater public savings) by relying on the private sector and improving the quality of services to consumers. The Royal Decree of June 1996 sets out the basic principles for greater reliance on the private sector, including the power industry, for which the government is moving ahead with full concessioning. The most notable offering to the private sector is in Salalah covering generation, transmission, and distribution, including the establishment of a new 200MW plant.

Oman also has the distinction of setting up the first private power generating plant in the Gulf. The Al-Manah Plant, set up in 1994, is selling electricity to the national power grid owned by the public sector and managed by the Ministry of Electricity and Water under a 20-year Power Purchasing Agreement (PPA). The Al-Manah project demonstrated the attractiveness of the Gulf to private sector operators and the government was able to get a "reasonable" price. However, the government now has to pay higher explicit production subsidies to Al-Manah than those required for public sector operators, and there is some concern over the apparently high cost of private capital.[2] Although some of the higher apparent costs are due to their being explicit – as opposed to the many hidden costs in public projects – a view persists that public capital may have been cheaper.

Oman has not initiated any privatizations in the gas or petroleum sector.

KUWAIT

Kuwait has the most wide-ranging privatization program in the Gulf. Between 1994 and 1996, the Kuwait Investment Authority (KIA) sold its major stakes in 17 companies covering the financial sector, real estate, manufacturing, and services.[3] The privatization program employed a variety of techniques, including the sale of shares to mutual funds that are also open to foreigners, direct sale through public auction (e.g., National

Industries and Gulf Insurance), public subscription (e.g., 70 million shares of Commercial Facilities Company), and direct sale in the stock exchange (small stakes of less than ten percent). The diversity of tools has allowed KIA to take advantage of the inclinations of the various investors in the market. Government revenue from the sale of these 17 firms has been about US$1.7 billion, while the receipts from the overall program have been greater than US$2 billion.

While Kuwait has been at the forefront of privatization in the Gulf, it has not privatized any infrastructure, utility, or energy sector enterprises. The Ministry of Electricity and Water is responsible for the production and distribution of electricity, which is 100 percent owned by the government. The Kuwait Petroleum Corporation (KPC) is also fully government-owned and has many subsidiaries that can be privatized, e.g., Koil Tanker Co., National Petroleum Company Refining, Kuwaiti Petroleum International (downstream operations), Kuwait Aviation Fuel Company, and retail outlets.

SAUDI ARABIA

Saudi Arabia has a relatively small state-enterprise sector as a proportion of GDP. However, public enterprises play an important role in the oil and petrochemicals sector, telecommunications, aviation, transport, water, and ports, and have a significant stake in the electricity enterprises. The Kingdom is formally initiating major privatization transactions, and private sector participation of various types is being pursued in ports, water, solid waste, health, toll roads, and other areas. The cabinet has recently approved privatization as a policy, and preparatory studies have been undertaken. As a follow-up to the cabinet decision, an inter-ministerial committee is expected to study the various issues in detail, develop an implementation plan, and initiate transactions. Some of the large utilities would need to go through a corporatization phase before they can be privatized. In telecommunications, the corporatization process was completed in an accelerated manner, and privatization options are being evaluated currently.

In the energy sector, Saudi Aramco is considered a strategic enterprise which is already managed on a commercial basis with private sector involvement. It is unlikely to be a candidate for privatization.

The electricity sector consists of four major utilities, called Saudi Consolidated Electricity Companies (SCECOs), in the eastern, western, central, and southern regions. A public utility operates eight generation stations in the northern region, which is also served by six other smaller private generation, distribution, and transmission companies. The sector has grown from 344MW in 1970 to almost 18,000MW in 1995, a growth rate of 17.8 percent annually. These SCECOs are owned jointly by the government and the private sector (as shares), and their shares are traded on the stock exchange. The sector is thus already "privatized," although the government could sell its stake in the SCECOs.

The government is considering options for dealing with some of the chronic problems facing the sector, such as tariffs that do not reflect full costs of production, build-up of arrears, and the need to restructure in order to improve efficiency. An electricity conservation policy is also in the preliminary stages.

The long-term financing need, reported to be US$117 billion over the next 25 years, is very large, and the government would have to look to the private sector for the future growth of the industry. Thus, one would expect private sector activity in the development of new projects in the sector, although it is unclear if the existing government stake in the SCECOs will be privatized any time soon.

UNITED ARAB EMIRATES

The UAE has an active private sector that plays an important role in the economy. However, the UAE only recently began a program of infrastructure privatization to promote further efficiency and enhance the role of the private sector. The federally-owned communication company, Etisalat, has announced plans to allow non-UAE companies to invest in the newly-formed Thurayya Satellite Communication Company. The Emirate of Ajman has signed a contract with an American firm to set up and operate a power station.

A new permanent committee was set up in May 1997 in Abu Dhabi to oversee the privatization of the state-owned Water and Electricity Department (WED). Rising demand in water and electricity is forcing the Dubai government to look at alternative financing. However, it is unclear if the Dubai Water and Electricity authority is looking for private investments. UAE-wide consolidation of the grid may be an issue as there are currently four utilities.

BAHRAIN

While Bahrain has a well-developed private sector and is counting on that sector to provide employment opportunities for its citizens, in recent years there has been relatively little privatization activity. Petroleum extraction and refining are owned by the government, and it is intended that they remain so. Similarly, electricity, water, and public transport remain as departments of government.

In contrast, however, there is a vigorous tourism industry largely in the hands of the private sector. In fact, the divestiture of government-held shares that took place in the late 1980s was primarily in this sector. The government is, however, the sole owner of the country's best hotel, the Meridien, which was built for a GCC Heads of State Meeting when it became clear that the private sector was unwilling to invest funds of the necessary magnitude.

Moreover, there is a large and healthy off-shore banking industry in Bahrain, entirely in private hands. The domestic banking industry is mostly private, although the government holds shares in the Housing Bank, the Bahrain Development Bank (BDB), and the National Bank of Bahrain. The domestic banking sector is weak, thus protected from competition with the off-shore banks, and tends to be very conservative in its lending practices.

The government is a partner with other GCC governments in the aluminum smelter (ALBA), the petrochemicals industry (GPIC), Gulf Air, and Arab Shipbuilding and Repair Yards (ASRY). It holds 80 percent of the shares in the aluminum extrusion company (BALEXCO), and one-third of the shares in the telecommunications company (BATELCO), a well-run and very successful private enterprise. Other share holdings include some food companies and a ten percent share of the local private monopoly in cement imports (NIXCO).

The 1992 census of establishments indicated some 2300 industrial (mining, manufacturing, and electricity) enterprises of ten or more employees. Of these, six were fully government-owned, and another ten were jointly held.

QATAR

Of all the Gulf states, Qatar has perhaps the largest state role in its economy. Apart from the oil and gas sector, state enterprises exist in fertilizer, insurance, banking, electricity, water, and other sectors. However, Qatar

Airways is privately owned. Although some of the ventures involve the private sector, there have been few moves towards privatization. It is possible that the government may initiate some limited privatization in the non-oil and gas sector, which is considered strategic.

Qatar has been successful in raising its offshore production over the last two years mainly because the government was able to attract international oil companies through oil sharing production.

Qatar Liquefied Gas Company (QATARGAS),[4] the majority state-owned liquefied natural gas (LNG) producer was successful in developing gas reserves for sale as LNG to Asian markets. The first export shipment to Japan was announced at the end of 1996. Also RasGas, another majority state-owned company, was able to raise US$1.2 billion in bonds internationally last year.

Annual growth in electricity demand is very high, around 11 percent a year. The Ministry of Electricity and Water is about to commission the construction of a 700MW power plant. A private company, Qatar Electricity and Water Company, created in the early 1990s to build and operate power plants, has not been successful so far.

Reasons for Continuing Government Involvement and Slow Privatization

There are several explanations for the continuing role of government and limited privatization activity in the Gulf. Historically, the role of the government in the countries of the Gulf was fashioned by four factors which contributed to the greater role of public enterprises in the economy:

- The large oil sectors were under public ownership;
- The availability of vast oil incomes meant that the fiscal constraints on government expenditures were relatively relaxed and concerns with efficiency of resource use were not paramount. Governments were therefore able to sustain large subsidies for public enterprises;
- Enormous infrastructure needs and programs also created a role for public financing and participation, particularly in the major utilities; and
- The government's desire to share the benefits of the oil rents led to subsidized provision of services including electricity.

In spite of the four reasons cited above, the ideology of the Gulf countries was, and remains, private sector oriented. As a result, the proportion of non-oil GDP emanating from the state enterprise sector is small by international standards.[5] Therefore, given the small base of public enterprise in the non-oil sector, the overall scope for privatization is limited. Even under a very active policy, privatization would be on a smaller scale than in many countries of Latin America, Asia, or Africa with large PE sectors.

Concern for Rising Prices: The Tariff Regime

The countries of the Gulf have generally used their public enterprises as instruments for the distribution of the oil rents. This has meant that the pricing of public utilities – specifically that of electric power – has been subsidized. Table 2.1 presents the electricity tariffs of the six GCC countries; Table 2.2 compares these tariffs with those of the world, illustrating that tariffs in the Gulf are amongst the lowest in the world. The electricity tariff of Kuwait (US$0.7 per kilowatt hour) is probably the lowest in the world, with Saudi Arabia not too far behind. For Qatari citizens,

Table 2.1
Current Electricity Charges in GCC

	UAE			Bahrain			Saudi Arabia		
	kW/hr	LC[1]	US$	kW/hr	LC[1]	US$	kW/hr	LC[1]	US$
Residential	any	7.5	(0.0204)	0–2,000	8	(0.016)	1–4,000	5	(0.013)
				2,000–5,000	12	(0.032)	4,001–6,000	8	(0.021)
				>5,000	16	(0.043)	>6,000	15	(0.040)
Commercial	any	7.5	(0.0204)	any	16	(0.0204)	1–4,000	5	(0.013)
							4,001–6,000	8	(0.021)
							>6,000	15	(0.040)

	Oman			Qatar[2]			Kuwait		
	kW/hr	LC[1]	US$[2]	kW/hr	LC[1]	US$[2]	kW/hr	LC[1]	US$[2]
Residential	0–3,000	10	(0.026)	0–4,000	6	(0.0175)			
	3,000–5,000	15	(0.038)	>4,000	8	(0.022)	1	2	(0.70)
	5,001–7,000	20	(0.052)						
	7,001–10,000	25	(0.065)						
	>10,000	30	(0.070)						
Commercial	any	20	(0.052)	0–4,000	6	(0.0175)	1	2	(0.70)
				4,000–15,000	8	(0.022)			
				>15,000	10	(0.028)			

Notes
1 LC = local currency.
2 In Qatar electricity is free for Nationals.

electricity is free for residential use. One of the consequences of these low tariffs has been high rates of consumption and limited conservation of electricity. Another consequence has been that the financial situation of the electricity companies is often precarious, and they are reliant upon regular infusions from the government to sustain themselves. In addition to the low level of tariff, the structure of tariffs is inconsistent with international practice. For example, the base range (subsistence) in OECD countries is between 100 and 200 kW/hrs, whereas the average for the Gulf is 4000–5000 kW/hrs.

Table 2.2
Average Prices of Power
Real 1990 US$ per Kilowatt Hour
Estimated Average Electricity Prices

	1984	1992–94[1]
Australia	0.05	0.0802[2]
Canada	0.0315	0.049
China	0.019	0.0280
France	0.06	0.01015
Germany	0.065	0.0135
India	0.0745	0.0356
Indonesia	0.01495	0.0579
Italy	0.0745	0.0126
Japan	0.01105	0.0211
Malaysia	0.01031	0.0651
Mexico	0.034	0.0555
New Zealand	0.024	0.0515
Norway	0.0275	0.067
Pakistan	0.0649	0.0661
Philippines	0.01369	0.0798
South Korea	0.01183	0.0646
Sweden	0.0335	0.061
Taiwan	0.0811	0.093
Thailand	0.01006	0.0622
Turkey	0.047	0.0765
United Kingdom	0.0575	0.0955
United States	0.0752	0.0624
Venezuela	0.043	0.032
Vietnam	n/a	0.053

Notes

1 For these countries, the most current price listed is for 1992 and is computed using nominal prices in local currency updated with local GDP deflators and converted using a nominal US dollar exchange rate. All other country prices are computer by the IEA using local currency, domestic energy price indices, and nominal US dollar exchange rates.

2 Estimated.

Source: IEA, Asian Development Bank, International Finance Corporation.

Concern for Domestic Employment

Another commonly cited explanation for the reluctance of Gulf governments to fully privatize their public enterprises, particularly the large ones, is fear that it will contribute to unemployment, at least in the short run. High population growth rates and rising education levels have increased the number of participants in the work force, creating fears of rising unemployment. This factor, combined with the presence of large expatriate populations, has led to efforts by almost all the Gulf countries to create more job openings for the domestic population. Traditionally, government ministries and public enterprises have been used to increase the levels of employment for the domestic workforce with the result that public enterprises are often over-staffed and have high ratios of domestic to foreign workers. It is a concern that the private sector, motivated primarily by commercial considerations, may reduce the levels of employment and may not be as amenable to recruiting higher proportions of domestic workers.

"Control," "Security," and "Strategic Sectors" Arguments

It is often argued that certain industries should remain under government ownership because they are "strategic" or because they are vital to the "security" of the country. Different countries adopt their own notion of what is classified as an industry that is strategic or vital for security. In the Gulf, this argument is used mostly in justifying government ownership of oil, natural gas, and other related industries and, in certain instances, firms operating in the financial sector and even major utilities such as telecommunications, water, and electricity.[6]

The Gulf War Postponed Reform

The 1990–91 Gulf War diverted the attention of policy makers, and reform of the economies was "put on hold." It had disastrous consequences and only now is the region beginning to recover from the adverse effects, fiscal or otherwise. It also reinforced the arguments for control and "security" discussed above. On the other hand, postwar austerity is forcing Gulf governments to rethink certain policies, including the continuation of subsidies and the role of the state in the economy.

Regional Dynamics

Privatization started in the 1980s and 1990s and was implemented with zeal in Great Britain, New Zealand, and the East European countries. It spread to Latin America where Chile, Argentina, Mexico, Peru, and others have implemented it as part of their economic reforms. Although it has now been adopted by many countries in Asia and even Africa, it has been slow in coming to the Middle East where, apart from Morocco, few countries have any real programs. Table 2.3 shows the almost non-existence of privatization in the Middle East. The region, including the Gulf countries, has therefore not felt either the "regional competition" on this front or the "demonstration effect" of a successful program.

The Case for Privatization

EFFICIENCY OF PRIVATE OWNERSHIP

The general case for privatization rests on the higher relative efficiency of private compared to public ownership. This case is based on both theory and empirical evidence. Many types of theoretical argument are provided in support of the higher relative efficiency of private ownership. The primary argument is that the government ("principal") must rely upon some bureaucrat ("agent") to manage the company, and a "principal-agent" problem arises because agents pursue their own interests while sacrificing those of the principal.

The problem is compounded by the lack of clear objectives, inadequate evaluation, defective incentives, and imposition of non-commercial objectives on the enterprises.

Many studies that compare the performance of firms under public and private ownership find that those under private ownership generally perform better. More recent studies that have compared the performance of firms before and after their privatization find that performance after privatization improves on a variety of indicators.[7]

FINANCING OF INFRASTRUCTURE

The infrastructure needs of Gulf countries are increasing. Although the Gulf countries, unlike some oil producers, have done a good job of transforming their oil wealth into impressive infrastructure, meeting future needs is going to be difficult unless private sources of financing are sought.

In the power sector alone, the additional financing needs are enormous. Table 2.4 gives an estimate of the power sector costs for the Gulf countries up to the year 2006. These estimates surpass US$30 billion and clearly require private sector participation. While BOO/BOT schemes can be tried, these tend to be resource and time intensive. It is generally easier to privatize an existing public enterprise by adding an investment require-ment from the private sector. In Sri Lanka, for example, a 51 percent stake in the Colombo Gas company was sold to Shell. In addition, the firm was also required to build a new terminal and inject US$40 million in new investment.

Table 2.3
Number of Infrastructure Privatizations and Estimated
Total Value by Region up to February 1997

	Gas	Power	Telecom	Transport	Waste	Water	Total	Total (US$ billion)
Sub-Saharan Africa	0	10	10	22	1	10	53	1.8
East Asia (Emerging Markets)	2	8	9	6	2	0	27	95.7
East Asia (Developed)	1	23	9	17	1	0	51	14.1
Western Europe	3	42	25	26	17	22	135	138.4
Eastern Europe/CIS	4	15	7	2	6	5	39	7.3
Latin America & Caribbean	13	65	23	37	7	6	151	50.3
Middle East & North Africa	2	0	2	0	0	1	5	0.6
North America	6	6	116	3	24	11	166	12.6
South Asia	0	2	1	1	0	0	4	1.4
Total	31	171	202	114	58	55	631	322.2

Source: World Bank paper "Infrastructure Privatization in the Middle East and North Africa" by Jamal Saghir.

Table 2.4
Gulf Power Requirements to 2006

Country	Projected cost[1] (US$ billion)	Demand growth rate (%)	Additional capacity by 2006[2]	Installed generating capacity (MW)
Bahrain	1.0	5.3	560	1,188
Kuwait	3.6	7.0	5,000	6,680
Oman	0.6	3.0	1,075	1,692
Qatar	1.6	11.6	1,400	1,900
Saudi Arabia	20.0	5.5	13,400	21,558
UAE	5.5	10.0	5,000	6,850

Notes

1 Estimated cost of planned additions.
2 Estimated additional capacity installed.

Source: *Middle East Economic Digest (MEED)*.

THE FISCAL CONSTRAINTS ARE LIKELY TO REMAIN

Privatization will be increasingly required in the Gulf in order to improve the fiscal situation and gain control of the public finances. The relatively tight fiscal situation is unlikely to improve for the Gulf countries.

The fiscal effects of privatizations work in many different ways. However, they are generally positive because privatization diminishes operational subsidies and government's capital expenditures, and increases government tax revenues.

FOCUS GOVERNMENT RESOURCES ON SOCIAL AND HUMAN RESOURCE DEVELOPMENT

The resources of the government are best spent in areas where the private sector may be unwilling to enter, but where the social gains are great. In the case of the Gulf, the big challenge is creating job opportunities for the domestic population. This policy of generating jobs can be accomplished either by making foreigners more costly to hire or by increasing the relative productivity of national workers. Clearly the second course is preferable, especially for long run sustained development. To achieve this end, Gulf governments would have to spend more of, and better utilize, their resources on human development and education. By privatizing areas where alternative funds are available (e.g., energy), governments will be able to devote their own resources to areas such as education.

ENERGIZING THE PRIVATE SECTOR

The main engine of growth is the private sector. With globalization, greater competition, and stagnant incomes from oil, the challenge is for the Gulf countries to expand their private sectors into the non-oil sectors and to create productive employment opportunities. The privatization program will energize the private sector by increasing its participation in the economy.

SIGNALING

Privatization is a low cost way to signal to the rest of the world the serious intentions of the Gulf countries to reform their economies, to attract private capital, including that of their own nationals, held abroad, and to revise policies that have given a disproportionate role to the government in certain key sectors.

RESPONDING TO SOME CONCERNS

In developing the case for privatization, it is important to respond to some of the concerns of the governments, particularly those relating to the increase in the costs of power and the possibility of increased unemployment.

Tariff

First, current tariffs are out of line with actual costs. As a result, subsidies are required for the electricity companies. Second, conservation efforts become difficult due to low tariffs. Third, given the large proportions of non-nationals, the subsidies are also benefiting foreigners as there is no simple way to single out nationals. Privatization can be an occasion to revisit the wisdom of subsidizing power, particularly with the magnitude of the subsidies involved.

A final and most important purpose of privatization is that even if governments wish to keep tariffs low for whatever reason, they can still privatize and benefit from the efficiencies associated with private sector operation. Of course, the lower the tariffs, the lower will be government receipts from the privatization of the entities. In the extreme case that tariffs are kept so low as to make the privatized firms financially non-viable, the government would have to subsidize private sector operators rather than public sector ones. The advantage, however, is that the subsidy is explicit, and the cost of pursuing this policy known to policy makers.

Employment

The fear that privatization will create unemployment of nationals in the short-term may be well-founded because public sector firms are usually overstaffed, and the Gulf is no different from other countries in this respect. The policy of generating employment via overstaffing public enterprises is inefficient; the costs of this policy are hidden, and it provides excuses for public enterprise managements to pursue inefficient practices. However, if the governments wish to keep the firms overstaffed for political reasons, the privatization can be designed to prevent the private firms from firing the workers for a period of time, as was done in the case of Colombo Gas. Alternately, employees can be given training and golden handshakes.

EASE OF PRIVATIZATION

Unlike some countries and regions such as Africa, privatization in the Gulf should be easier to accomplish once the governments have decided to move. There are several reasons for this. First, as domestic private capital is available, fears of foreign domination are unlikely to be strong. Given the ideological bent and the small size of most Gulf countries, this issue is unlikely to be important except in two or three countries. Second, the Gulf countries are not perceived as risky by the international investor community. Thus, a program of privatization is likely to receive favorable reactions from international investors. Third, they can afford the upfront costs.

Some Relevant Issues for Energy Privatization in the Gulf

While there are some issues related to privatization that are applicable to all or most Gulf countries, the strategy for each country must be specific and tailored to its particular circumstances. This section will highlight some issues that Gulf countries will need to resolve if they want to successfully move forward with the privatization of their enterprises in the energy sector.

LEGAL RESTRUCTURING AND CORPORATIZATION

A key strategic question facing Gulf countries is the type and degree of restructuring prior to privatization. Restructuring can take many forms including organizational, employee, legal, and financial. In some Gulf countries, the electricity firms, for example, are still government departments. Prior to privatization, they would need to go through a change of legal form (corporatization). This would entail creating separate accounts and balance sheets and redefining the relationship between the parent ministry and the corporatized entity.

EMPLOYEE RESTRUCTURING

Given the over-staffing in the energy public enterprises of some Gulf countries, privatization would require an explicit policy. There are several options. The first is to reduce the number of employees using golden handshakes or voluntary redundancy prior to privatization. If this is viewed as unacceptable, then the ministries can be asked to absorb the surplus employees as part of the corporatization process, where this option is available. Third, the enterprises can be privatized with the employees, and the new owners given the right to terminate their services after a period of time, or to let the growth of the enterprises take care of the surplus. A final – perhaps least desirable option – would be to have a clause in the privatization contract that forces the firms to keep all the employees.

TARIFFS

As discussed above, current tariffs in the Gulf countries are out of line with costs, and some of the enterprises may not be commercially viable in the absence of subsidies. Privatization would require rethinking the wisdom of such pricing policies. Post-privatization tariff regimes would need to be explicitly defined, with either the governments revising tariffs upward or agreeing to explicit subsidies.

COMPETITION AND INDUSTRY STRUCTURE

The privatization of a monopoly utility is like privatizing the entire sector. Thus questions of the industry structure become important. A related issue is that privatization is not an end in itself, but rather a means towards improving the efficiency of the energy sector. For efficiency, competition is as important as ownership; some would say even more important. Therefore, the issue of determining the structure of the sector, and the manner in which the sector is restructured, broken up, or unbundled is important. For example, in England and Wales, the electricity sector was restructured into a National Grid Company (NGC), two power generating companies (National Power and PowerGen), and 12 regional electricity companies prior to privatization. In Argentina, the power sector was broken up into generating, transmission, and distribution activities. The generation part itself was broken up into 20 separate companies and sold to private firms to promote competition. Because of this competition, wholesale electricity prices fell significantly. The Argentinean gas monopoly, GDE, was broken up into two transmission and eight distribution companies. The oil monopoly YPF was completely restructured; its strategic functions were separated from the non-strategic ones and these were further broken into many firms and sold separately. Hungary unbundled its power sector into seven generating, one trans-mission, and six distribution companies as part of the privatization.[8]

INTER-ENTERPRISE AND GOVERNMENT ARREARS

Like in many other countries, government energy enterprises in the Gulf also have problems with collecting their bills from government agencies and departments who are major users of energy. The existing backlog of arrears would require some solution and the future rules of the game would have to be specified.

THE "STRATEGIC" SECTORS ISSUE

It is important for governments to determine their role in the oil sector and what type of privatization, if any, to pursue. It is difficult for technical experts to respond to arguments for a continuing role of government as a producer in an industry, because the industry is described as "strategic." The strategic industry argument can be used to justify the public owner-ship of virtually any industry including rice and wheat production. In dealing with the issue of strategic industry, the Gulf countries should also consider the relevance of the "golden share" whereby the government retains a veto on key decisions of the privatized company. The golden share has been used by several countries.

REGULATION

A major reason for government ownership of infrastructure enterprises, particularly those operating in monopolies, is the fear that the private sector will abuse its market power by reducing the quality of service or increasing prices. Privatization will only lead to an increase in the welfare of society if it is accompanied by government regulation of the privatized utilities. There are many lessons of international experience in the estab-lishment and rules of regulation; Gulf countries will have to invest in and work hard to adopt the best practical models of regulation. This will require government resources and commitment.

ROLE OF FOREIGNERS

In the case of the Gulf countries, domestic private capital exists in sufficiently large quantities that, if the governments chose, foreigners could be kept out of the purchase of energy enterprises. However, there is strong evidence from privatization elsewhere that bringing in reputable international groups as partners in consortiums or joint

ventures with domestic parties will provide the technology and management expertise that may otherwise be absent. This issue would need to be
resolved.

INSTITUTIONAL AND IMPLEMENTATION CAPACITY

Privatization programs require careful design and tailoring to the local
situation. Many government decisions and implementation steps are
involved. For these transactions to be completed in a transparent way and
lead to socially desirable outcomes, it is necessary to create the decision-
making apparatus and implementation machinery which is currently
lacking in Gulf countries. Since much of the work can be contracted out
to international experts, limited in-house capability will be required.
Nevertheless, this capability is critical and needs full government commitment without which progress will be difficult and the policy itself
could be discredited.

CHAPTER 3

The Legal Framework for Privatization in the United Arab Emirates

Andrew Ward

Introduction

Privatization has been much talked about in the Middle East for a number of years, particularly in the Gulf. The true catalysts for privatization vary, of course, from country to country, depending largely on the economic and historical circumstances of the country in question. However, governments will usually attribute a decision to privatize to one or more of the following:

- Improving the efficient operation of public assets and services;
- Raising money for the government or reducing government expenditure;
- Stimulating capital market development and thereby widening investment opportunities for the private sector;
- Freeing enterprises such as public utilities from the investment constraints inherent in government finances; and
- Introducing competition in undertakings previously carried out by state-owned monopolies.

Of course, all of these reasons are interlinked, and it is ultimately a matter of emphasis as to what is the primary reason for a particular country to embark on a privatization program. That said, a shortage of finance can focus a government on the desirability of privatization and prompt its rapid implementation. Perhaps it is the wealth of the UAE which led many commentators, even just a few years ago, to dismiss the likelihood of any significant privatization in the UAE. Indeed, even after the creation in Abu Dhabi of a committee to study the possible privatization of the Emirate's WED, there was skepticism among national and expatriate communities in the UAE as to whether privatization would occur.

However, in May 1997 following the initial studies, the Abu Dhabi government decided to establish a permanent committee, under the Chairmanship of His Highness Sheikh Dhiyab Bin Zayed Al Nahyan, with the mandate to privatize the WED. Suddenly it became clear that the Abu Dhabi government had indeed embraced the concept of privatization.[1] The Abu Dhabi Privatization Committee's tasks effectively encompass both the unbundling and privatization of parts of the existing WED as well as the future procurement of new capacity through independent water and power producers. Substantial annual increases in demand in both sectors make the commissioning of new plants a priority, and the Committee has already begun the challenging task of implementing its brief.

Although the scope of this chapter is more general than the legal issues facing the Privatization Committee in its work, inevitably it will use, by way of example, certain aspects of the UAE's first major infrastructure privatization program.

What Is Meant by Privatization?

Privatization has no strict legal definition. In its widest sense, almost any process which involves the private sector in operating or investing in publicly-owned assets or providing services previously provided by public bodies can be referred to as privatization. The possible methods of privatization range from various forms of public asset sales through the introduction of private management skills and disciplines without any change in ownership, to the contracting out of services previously provided by the state. Thus, privatization can encompass any of the following examples:

- The unbundling of a vertically integrated state-owned monopoly utility and the sale of shares in the various resulting companies to the public by way of one or more initial public offerings (IPOs);
- The sale of shares in existing government-owned ventures to private investors by way of private contract;
- The philanthropic transfer, free of charge, of shares in state-owned companies to less wealthy nationals;
- The financing and operation of infrastructure projects through BOOT schemes;
- Introducing private sector management to a state-owned enterprise

through a management services agreement (whether with or without the management acquiring a stake in the enterprise itself); and

- At its most basic, the contracting of services to the private sector, such as hospital cleaning or laundry services, previously carried out by public servants.

The legal framework and the laws required to implement privatization will differ depending on the type of privatization carried out. For example, laws relating to the formation and ownership of companies will not be of primary importance when a management services agreement is contemplated (unless an equity incentive scheme is used). On the other hand, the law relating to companies will be crucial in structuring a privatization program involving the sale of shares in a state-owned enterprise to the private sector.

That said, it is possible to set out some very basic legal requirements, the existence of which may have a significant impact on the success of any privatization program.

The Basic Legal Requirements

Privatization cannot happen unless the private sector is willing to participate. The legal system which governs the privatization process itself and the rights of the private sector thereafter will inevitably impact on the decision of its members to participate and, if so, on what terms. In order to provide the optimum conditions for successful privatization, the laws and institutions of the privatizing state will need to provide authority for the privatization process, a stable system of business laws, and a dispute resolution mechanism.

AUTHORITY FOR PRIVATIZATION PROCESS

It goes without saying that a privatization program is unlikely to proceed in the optimum manner if there is doubt as to the authority of the privatizing government or other institutions to effect the privatization process. It must be clear that the government has the right to sell the assets which it is proposing to sell. In some Arab countries (although not the UAE), specific legislation is required before any public asset can be sold. Furthermore, in countries (typically former socialist states) where enterprises which are now to be privatized were previously expropriated from private ownership, the rights of former owners must be considered.

A STABLE SYSTEM OF BUSINESS LAWS

Investors, particularly foreign investors, will require legal certainty. Otherwise, they cannot quantify the risk which they are taking in entering into any particular privatization transaction. Thus, the existence of clear laws governing the essential elements of investment and conducting business, particularly laws concerning property rights, contracts, mortgages, companies, and currency convertibility and repatriation will be required.

A DISPUTE RESOLUTION MECHANISM

Investors and contractors will want to be sure that contracts which they (or the company in which they are investing) enter into will be enforced in the manner intended at the outset. Typically, such contracts will include a clause stating the parties' preferred method of dispute resolution. This could require arbitration either in or outside the privatizing state or submission to the jurisdiction of the courts of a country which may or may not be the privatizing state. Ultimately, even an arbitration award or a foreign court judgment, if not complied with, must be enforced by a court. Therefore, it is important that parties entering into contracts which will have to be enforced in a privatizing state can rely on an impartial and commercially sophisticated judicial system.

A Brief Description of the UAE's Legal Framework

Before analyzing how particular aspects of UAE law might affect certain types of privatization methods, it is important to consider how the legal system is structured, as this may have a considerable impact on the freedom of a privatizing government to pass new laws to facilitate the privatization process.

The UAE is a federal state; under the Constitution, the federal government (which is comprised of representatives from all seven Emirates – Abu Dhabi, Dubai, Sharjah, Ras Al-Khaimah, Fujairah, Umm Al-Qaiwain, and Ajman) has exclusive legislative jurisdiction in a number of areas.[2] The individual emirates have jurisdiction in those matters not assigned to the exclusive jurisdiction of the federal government (see Figure 3.1).[3]

Figure 3.1
UAE's Legal Framework

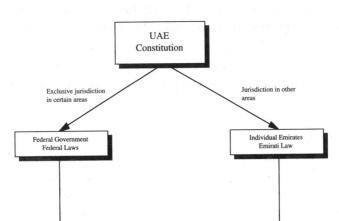

Since, in practice, most privatizations – such as Abu Dhabi's proposed water and electricity sector privatization – are likely to involve the privatization by individual emirates of public assets owned by or services provided within the emirate in question, it should be borne in mind that the relevant Emirati government, while it will be free to amend its own laws in order to facilitate the privatization, will have to structure it within the constraints of federal law.

Among the matters over which the federal government has jurisdiction are the laws relating to companies and civil and commercial transactions (including the law of contract).[4] Accordingly, the major business laws which will impact on the structuring of privatization in any of the emirates are federal laws, such as the Federal Law on Commercial Companies (the Companies Law), the Commercial Transactions Code, and the Civil Code.[5]

In relation to the energy sector, the natural resources of each emirate fall within its own jurisdiction and each emirate retains control of its own oil and gas resources. There are no federal laws relating to crude oil or gas. However, the Constitution includes electricity (but not water) services among the matters over which the federal government has exclusive legislative and executive jurisdiction.[6] Indeed, there is a Federal Ministry of Electricity and Water which was established by federal law shortly after the establishment of the UAE.[7] It is responsible for carrying out water and electricity projects and for the management and operation of water and electricity infrastructure to the extent that they fall within the federal government budget. It also has regulatory powers with respect to the electricity sector. At first sight, this would appear to have major implications for Abu Dhabi's water and electricity sector privatization program. However, under a transitional provision in the Constitution, Abu Dhabi's own WED has retained ownership and control of its electricity and water production, transmission, and distribution assets. Indeed, both Dubai and Sharjah provide for their own water and electricity needs.[8] Thus, in practice, the functions of the Federal Ministry of Water and Electricity apply only in the four northern emirates and its jurisdiction only extended to Ras Al Khaimah in 1991 when that emirate so requested and its own WED was subsumed into the Federal Ministry.

This situation illustrates the complexity of the inter-relationship between federal and Emirati law. The likelihood of the federal government seeking to assert authority over the electricity functions in the Emirate of Abu Dhabi against the wishes of the Abu Dhabi government is negligible. However, one can imagine the legal advisers of a proposed foreign investor or contractor in Abu Dhabi's privatization program spending hours worrying over this issue.

There is one further general point regarding the UAE legal framework insofar as it affects privatization. Unsurprisingly, in view of the background outlined above, the UAE has no privatization law. A general privatization law is, of course, not essential for a privatization transaction. Indeed, Oman remains the only GCC country with a law which sets out the principles and guidelines governing privatization in the state. In the absence of such a law, when structuring the privatization it is, of course, necessary to take into account the various existing laws which may be of relevance to the particular transaction in question.

Having established that there is no privatization law and that the laws which will be of importance in any privatization will vary according to its nature, it may, therefore, be instructive to look at two common methods of privatization – both of which are likely to be used by the Abu Dhabi Privatization Committee – and to identify some of the legal issues which are likely to arise from the current UAE legal system. Accordingly, this chapter will initially consider the legal framework insofar as it may affect the provision of new infrastructure through private sector financing and operation and secondly, the way in which the privatization of existing public assets through their sale or transfer to the private sector may fall within the existing legal framework and what new laws may have to be enacted in order to effect this.

Privately Financed Infrastructure Projects

In relation to the provision of new infrastructure through the private sector (as opposed to the privatization of existing infrastructure), it has become increasingly common for governments to use schemes in which the private sector is asked to finance the construction of the infrastructure in question and is then granted an operating concession – which may be of limited or unlimited duration – so that it can make enough money to finance and repay the debt incurred in connection with the project while making a reasonable return. These sorts of schemes have come to be known by a variety of related acronyms such as BOOT, BOT (build-operate-transfer), and BOO schemes. Essentially, BOOT and BOT refer to limited duration concessions (the reference to "transfer" being the transfer of the project to the government at the end of the concession) while BOO refers to a concession of unlimited duration.

The Abu Dhabi Privatization Committee has already announced that one of its first tasks will be to structure the planned Taweelah A Extension Cogeneration Plant as an Independent Water and Power Producer (IWPP) using a BOO scheme structure. All future major capacity expansions in the emirate will also be implemented as IWPPs.[9] Similarly, Dubai Investments has announced plans for a new privately financed and operated power station at Jebel Ali. Again, a BOO scheme will reportedly be used but this is not part of a wider scheme to privatize Dubai's electricity sector.

Generally, the structure for a project such as an IWPP involves a large number of interrelated legal documents involving a number of different parties which will effectively set out the regulatory framework within which the IWPP will operate and allocate the risks which might affect the project (whether commercial, market, or political) between the various parties. Every project is different, and there is no standard set of agreements which can be used. Figure 3.2 sets out an example of how an IWPP project may be structured.

Typically, a new company will be set up to carry out the project for the purpose of obtaining non-recourse finance. For this purpose, non-recourse financing means loans made to the project vehicle without any recourse on the part of the lenders to the assets of its shareholders. Thus Figure 3.2 shows two sources of financing for the project vehicle – investments by shareholders (who will typically include the operator and main contractor as well as others) under an equity investment agreement, and debt financing by lending banks under a non-recourse loan agreement. Banks will naturally wish to take security over the assets of the project vehicle, including its revenue streams under any supply contracts into which the project vehicle enters.

Figure 3.2
Project Vehicle Financing

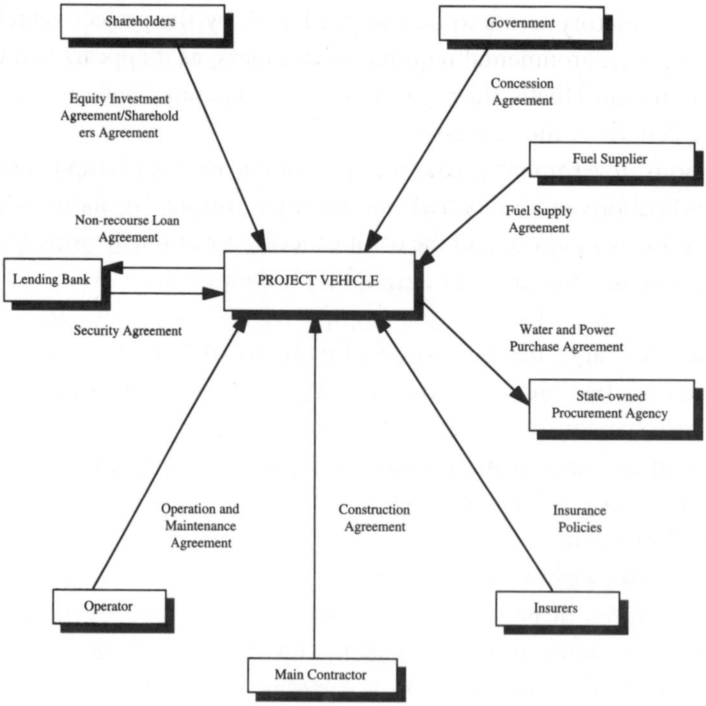

Because of the high level of sunk costs involved in the construction of infrastructure such as a power station, security over the project assets will be unlikely to provide sufficient comfort to potential lenders to make the project financially feasible. The key to a project's "bankability" will be the revenue stream generated by the project. In particular, lenders will wish to see a long-term fuel supply agreement under which the IWPP will receive a reliable supply of fuel, and a guarantee that the IWPP will be able to sell its product profitably to a creditworthy purchaser. Such a guarantee will be provided in the form of a long-term take or pay contract with a government-owned procurement agency. A take or pay contract is one in which the procurement agency guarantees it will pay for a minimum amount of the project's products, whether or not it takes delivery.

A further important element in the project's makeup is the involvement of government which is often set out in a concession agreement. Under this agreement, a variety of matters may be agreed upon between the government and the project vehicle and/or its shareholders. These may include:

- The grant of the necessary land for the project;
- The grant of all necessary licenses, consents, and approvals for the project, and the expedition of matters such as visas;
- The regulatory terms to be complied with by the project vehicle (for example environmental requirements) unless, as it appears will be the case in Abu Dhabi, these are set out in a separate regulatory law;
- The length of the concession; and
- Various government guarantees pertaining to, for example, currency convertibility and repatriation, taxation, future legislative changes affecting the project, and the compliance by government-owned entities (such as the procurement agency) with their contracts.

Other key agreements shown in Figure 3.2 include:

- The construction agreement with the main contractor which is likely to be a fixed price turnkey agreement;
- The operation and maintenance agreement with the operator of the IWPP which will be designed to incentivize the efficient operation of the IWPP; and
- The policies provided by insurers.

Thus, it can be seen that the success or otherwise of such a project hinges on the negotiation of a large number of contracts among a host of parties, with government and its institutions playing a pivotal role. Ultimately, as with any freely negotiated bargain, the project will only proceed if the various parties to it are satisfied that the potential rewards outweigh the risks (including any risks arising out of the legal environment surrounding the project). Considering the structure outlined above in the context of the UAE legal framework, there are a number of points which may have an effect on the structure itself and on the parties' assessment of the risk factors, including the structuring of the project vehicle, lender's security, contractual enforcement, and regulatory certainty.

Structuring the Project Vehicle

Any company formed in the UAE as the project vehicle must be formed under the Federal Companies Law. This law contains some requirements with which some foreign investors will not be familiar and which may restrict the freedom of the parties (including Emirati governments) to structure a project in the manner they might wish.

All UAE companies must be at least 51 percent owned by UAE nationals or 100 percent owned by UAE national-owned companies.[10] In the proposed Abu Dhabi IWPPs, it is anticipated that a 60 percent majority of IWPPs will be owned initially by the Abu Dhabi government. In other cases, in the absence of such government investment, UAE private sector investment will have to be sought. This will have a direct impact on the choice of the type of company which is to be used as the project vehicle as the Companies Law sets out several types of companies with a number of arbitrary rules which may dictate which form of company is to be used. For example, if a public offering of shares is required, the project vehicle will have to be a Public Joint Stock Company. This entails an IPO before the company is incorporated, and the rules laid down by the Companies Law as to what may happen if the offering is under-subscribed may make a traditional underwriting impossible.[11] At present, this is not a matter of great concern to local issuers as all offerings to date have been substantially oversubscribed, but it could cause concern to potential foreign investors. In circumstances where there are to be a limited number of shareholders, including perhaps an Emirati government, the preferred project vehicle may be a limited liability company (LLC). Although shareholders in joint stock companies also benefit from limited liability, the LLC is often seen as a more flexible investment vehicle for a limited number of investors. However, it should be remembered that any company in which the federal government or any of its institutions is to invest must be a public joint stock company.[12]

There is no distinction between authorized and issued share capital and, due to the statutory rules about new issues of shares, it can be difficult to structure equity incentive packages involving the future issue of new shares in the project vehicle. Furthermore, the Companies Law does not permit shares of different classes.[13] Thus, structures involving preferred stock or the like will not work.

The timing of forming the project vehicle will be important. Company formation can take a significant period of time, depending on the type of company used; shareholders will have unlimited liability for any transactions entered into prior to formation of the company.[14]

LENDER'S SECURITY

Any security taken by lenders to the project vehicle will have to be structured within the constraints of UAE laws. In practice, it is likely that lenders will be looking for security in the revenue stream of the IWPP and in those major assets in which security can be taken. Thus, the lenders may seek assignments of the revenue streams under the water and power purchase agreement, any liquid damages payable by the main contractor in the event of contractor default, and the proceeds of the insurance policies. Provided the various parties to those contracts are in agreement, there should be no great difficulty under UAE law in effecting the security.

Security over tangible assets may prove somewhat more difficult (although this may well not be crucial to the bankability of the project). In particular, although a law passed in Dubai in 1996 permits the mortgaging of land to banks for the purposes of financing construction, this is not the case elsewhere in the UAE. The Commercial Transactions Code makes provision for mortgages over moveable property to secure commercial debts but, for such mortgages to be effective, title to the mortgaged asset has to be transferred to the mortgagee along with possession (or at least joint possession) so that the mortgagor cannot dispose of the asset without the knowledge of the mortgagee.[15] Thus, the procedure may be somewhat impractical in the case of assets which are required for the day-to-day operation of the IWPP.

Furthermore, the Commercial Transaction Code provides for mortgages to be granted by companies over the whole of a "commercial house" (which is basically defined as being the assets required for carrying on commercial activities) provided that the mortgage deed is attested or certified by a notary public and the mortgage is entered in the commercial register.[16] The difficulty here is that, in Abu Dhabi, there is no register for such mortgages although steps are being taken to create one.

CONTRACTUAL ENFORCEMENT

As highlighted in Figure 3.2, the whole IWPP project hangs on a contractual matrix – the network of interrelated and interdependent contracts described earlier. A default by one of the parties under one of the agreements can lead to knock-on defaults by other parties under other agreements. For example, a default by the state-owned procurement agency in payment under the water and power purchase agreement could lead to the IWPP project vehicle defaulting under its loan arrangements, which could ultimately bring down the whole project. It is therefore most important to the various parties to have confidence that, in the event of a default, the contracts can be enforced in a timely manner in accordance with their terms.

Many foreign investors in infrastructure projects prefer to have the agreements which underlie any project made subject to a system of law and a means of dispute resolution with which they are familiar. Frequently this will involve the contracts being interpreted in accordance with the laws of a foreign country with disputes being resolved by arbitration in one of the major seats of international arbitration. The laws of the UAE do not prohibit parties from selecting a foreign law to govern their contracts and, subject to some exceptions, the laws of the UAE permit parties to choose arbitration as a means of dispute resolution. However, the Federal Civil Procedures Law contains certain conditions which must be satisfied before a UAE Court will enforce a foreign court or arbitration award such that, in practice, it is unlikely that such an award would be enforced by a UAE court when a party to the dispute is resident in the UAE or where the dispute relates to a contract which is to be performed in the UAE.[17] The UAE is not a signatory to the 1958 New York Convention on the Recognition and Enforcement of Foreign Arbitral Awards under which each signatory nation accepts binding obligations to prevent parties from litigating in its courts in breach of a valid arbitration agreement and to recognize and enforce arbitral awards from other states. All of these issues will be weighed up by potential investors as part of their assessment of risk and reward in relation to any particular project.

REGULATORY CERTAINTY

Obviously, the investors in a project can only take an informed decision as to whether to participate when they know what the rules of the game will be. As previously mentioned, it is for this reason that the agreements with the government will normally contain provisions relating to future changes in the law. For example, in a one-off project for the provision of a new power station, it is possible that the regulatory system within which the power station must operate can be set out in the government contracts. However, when a project forms part of a major privatization program, as is the case in Abu Dhabi, it is most likely that a new regulatory system will be introduced covering all aspects of the industry including generation, distribution, and supply. Obviously, it will be vital to have this system in place before proposals are requested from potential investors in the IWPP. It is for this reason that the Abu Dhabi Privatization Committee has set a very tight timetable for the formulation of a new regulatory system.

Privatization of Existing Public Undertakings

Turning to the subject of privatization of existing public undertakings through their transfer or sale to private investors, as previously mentioned, the UAE has no privatization law. Therefore, it is necessary to consider the existing UAE legal framework to see how this might impact on the government's privatization plans. There are neither constitutional nor legal prohibitions on an Emirati government disposing of assets which it owns. However, the legal framework which will be relevant to any particular privatization will depend on its nature. For example, the sale of shares in an existing government-owned company would be a good deal simpler than the unbundling of a government department and the sale of its parts to the private sector, as would be the case of the Abu Dhabi WED which operates a vertically integrated monopoly utility. In the first case, privatization may simply involve the sale of shares in the existing company to a private purchaser, or offering them to the public. In the latter case, before any assets can be sold, the entire industry must be restructured, the requisite assets transferred to the appropriate newly formed companies, potentially a new contractual matrix for the industry put in place, and new legislation passed to govern the way in which the various new players in the industry will operate, typically including an entirely new regulatory body to oversee the industry.

Essentially, the main reason for restructuring a state-owned monopoly utility before privatization is that part of it (but not all) can be categorized as a natural monopoly. For example, once an electricity transmission grid has been built in an area or a water or gas pipe laid down a street, it will not be economically feasible for a competing grid to be built or pipe laid. Nor indeed is it likely to be desirable – how many times should the public be inconvenienced by a street being dug up to lay pipes? Thus, the possibility of introducing competition, which is a natural stimulus to efficiency and lower prices, is unlikely in activities where there is a natural monopoly. There are, however, activities which can be competitive. Thus upstream activities such as electricity generation and water and gas production and downstream activities such as the supply of water, gas, and electricity to consumers can all be competitive. However, if the entity which carries out the natural monopoly function is also involved in competitive upstream or downstream activities, it will potentially have an unfair advantage over its competitors. Thus, it is preferable to have natural monopoly functions carried out by a separate entity (which can either be in government or private hands) which is required to treat all users of its infrastructure equally and fairly.

There are several reasons for the desirability of introducing, before privatization, a new regulatory system for the sector which is to be privatized. Obviously, one reason is to regulate the behavior of the body carrying out the natural monopoly function in the manner previously mentioned. In addition, it must be borne in mind that vertically integrated utilities and their privatized successors are the providers of essential public services which will usually also involve significant safety considerations. Thus, typically, the regulatory regime will also be aimed at providing protection to consumers both in relation to the prices they will have to pay and in relation to such matters as safety and continuity of supply. In other words, the regulatory regime will typically aim to provide a balance between the cost-cutting efficiencies promoted by privatization and the safety and reliability requirements of such a utility.

It is essential that the new regulatory regime be put in place before the sale of any part of the industry to the private sector. Without this, potential private sector players will not be able to judge the value of the businesses in which they are being asked to invest. Thus, in any emirate planning to privatize all or part of a vertically-integrated monopoly utility, before the privatization is effected, legislation will first have to be enacted for three main reasons:

- To transfer to the newly incorporated companies that are to take over the various functions of the utility, those assets and liabilities, including existing contracts, and those employees which are required to enable the new company to carry on its allotted business. (This, of course, is no easy task as the question of the division of assets and liabilities requires careful study and consideration, and issues such as the extent to which the new companies should be liable for such matters as pre-existing environmental contamination can have a significant impact on the willingness of the private sector to invest);

- To create a new regulatory body to supervise the industry and the new regulatory regime under which industry players will have to operate; and

- Potentially, to introduce a new contractual relationship between the various unbundled companies where there is no pre-existing contract. For example, the natural monopoly function of operating an electricity transmission grid will require the owner of the grid to have contracts with those using its system. In a vertically integrated utility, there will be no such contracts but they will have to be in place from the day on which the unbundling occurs. Thus it would not be unusual for the privatization legislation to introduce a series of deemed contracts between the new players in the industry. Any Emirati government seeking to introduce such a contractual matrix or, indeed, a regulatory system governing the contracts between the new industry players will have to take into account the requirements of the Federal Commercial Transactions Code, which itself sets out certain deemed contractual terms in the absence of a specific contract.

Another issue which any government will want to consider when privatizing an industry is the extent to which the government should retain some form of control following privatization. In a private sale, the government can insist on contractual protections to ensure that the newly privatized undertaking is operated in a manner which is consistent with government policy. However, where privatization is by means of a public offering, this is not possible. Accordingly, in many privatizations around the world, governments have retained a golden share which entrenches certain government rights in the constitution of the privatized company.

For example, golden shares have been used to:

- Restrict the levels of individual shareholdings in the company to a prescribed limit;
- Place limits on foreign shareholdings;
- Give government the right to veto actions by the company (for example the disposal of material parts of its business); and
- Allow government to appoint members of the Board of Directors.

Under the Federal Companies Law, however, it is not permitted to have different classes of shares in a company or for special rights to be attached to certain shares.[18] Thus, the traditional golden share route cannot be used in the UAE. As an alternative, it would be possible for a specific law (perhaps the Emiri Decree pursuant to which the company is set up) to impose certain legislative requirements for government consents.

Finally, it is important to note that the same issues under the Federal Companies Law which were referred to earlier, such as the difficulty of structuring traditional underwriting, will apply in the case of any public issue of shares in a privatized company.

Conclusion

There is currently no specifically designed legal framework for privatization in the UAE – no privatization law or the like has been passed. Thus, one must look at the possible methods of privatization in light of the existing legal framework. Unsurprisingly, any major privatization program will require the passing of new legislation by the privatizing government – this has been the case around the world. Any Emirati government which wishes to privatize will have to operate within the constraints imposed by federal law, some of which have been described. In addition, any privatization project will have to balance carefully the risks and rewards involved in the enterprise in question so as to ensure that the potential rewards for the private sector's participation are sufficient to justify its risk in doing so while still ensuring that the benefits of privatization in terms of greater efficiency and lower prices flow through to the government and the public. Undoubtedly, as is the case anywhere in the world, any major privatization in the UAE will involve very significant issues.

CHAPTER 4

The Indian Oil Experience: A Case Study

Leena Srivastava and Rajnish Goswami

Introduction

The hydrocarbons sector has played a critical role for several decades in meeting India's energy requirements. Recognizing the importance of this energy form – due both to its superior quality and lower environmental implications – the Government of India (GOI) is putting in place several measures to enhance participation, and thereby investment, in this sector as well as to ensure its sound financial viability. This chapter traces the role and progress of hydrocarbons in India's energy. It also presents scenarios of the likely supply and demand in the country, highlights major issues of concern, describes recent reform measures that have been put in place, and discusses regulatory changes that are likely to occur based on current driving forces.

India is very well endowed with coal resources and has in place coal reserves sufficient to last the country for the next 200 years at current rates of exploitation. However, despite being endowed with large sources of coal, hydropower, and other renewable energy, India finds itself faced with a high level of dependency on hydrocarbons and limited energy options for the future. In trying to cope with perennial energy and capital shortages, the country has consistently had to make sub-optimal choices in the development of energy resources. This, accompanied by the use of the energy sector as a vehicle for social largesse, has resulted in a situation today wherein the government must undertake major reform programs aimed at undoing the mistakes of the past. A major aim of the reform programs is to correct the basic flaw of subsidized energy provision which has resulted in the poor financial health of the energy providers.

Additionally, the government is now also adopting a more hands-off approach to managing the energy sector, thereby recognizing the role of the private sector and free markets.

Energy Demand

The pace and pattern of energy demand growth in India have been influenced to a large extent by the growth and structure of the economy, population growth, and the extent of urbanization. The Indian economy has historically been developed as a mixed economy dominated by the public sector. As such, the structure and growth of the economy have been influenced significantly by the allocation of plan budgets across various sectors.

The initial planning periods focused on industrial growth in a conscious attempt to improve the infrastructure base of the economy, with scant attention being paid to the agricultural sector. By the early sixties, however, it was apparent that India was heading for a food crisis, and the focus of planning shifted from industry to agriculture. In the Sixth Plan period (1980–85), a major redistributive change in the allocation of resources was apparent again, oriented towards achieving a high growth rate for the economy. Recognizing the supply of electricity as a crucial input to economic growth, the plan allocation for the power sector increased dramatically from roughly 18 percent to over 28 percent in this period.

At the time of independence, India was largely an agrarian economy with agriculture and allied activities contributing nearly 60 percent of the total GDP. However, by the end of the Seventh Plan period, the share of agriculture in GDP was down to 32 percent while the share of industry had increased from 15 percent in 1950–51 to nearly 30 percent. The share of the services sector, in particular transportation and communications, also increased significantly to meet the needs of an increasingly integrated domestic market and increased international trade.

India's population, largely dependent on agriculture, grew at an average annual rate of 2.15 percent between 1951 and 1991. However, the gross sown area over this period increased by a mere 0.8 percent. This, accompanied by a lack of developmental activity in rural areas, resulted in large scale migration to urban areas. The share of urban population in the total thereby increased from 17.3 percent in 1951 to 25.7 percent in 1991.

The Indian Energy Scene

The significant structural changes in the economy and population led to large increases in the consumption of commercial energy. However, the rural population in the country, despite various interventionist measures, continues to depend heavily on biomass fuels. Even today, these fuels are estimated to account for around 40 percent of the total national final energy consumption and 90 percent of the energy consumption in rural areas. However, the role of traditional fuels is decreasing as they are being increasingly substituted by more efficient commercial fuels, largely oil products.

India is relatively well endowed with both exhaustible and renewable energy resources. Coal is the major exhaustible energy resource of the country, and has a life expectancy of over 200 years. However, on a per capita basis, coal resources would still be well below the world average. As with other resources, this cannot be construed as a resource shortage per se but signifies an unequal distribution of resources in the world. Table 4.1 presents the proven energy resources in India and the total world resources.

Table 4.1
Proven Energy Resources

	Unit	India	World	India's world %
Coal	bmt	69.95	1031.60	6.8 %
Oil	Bbbl	4.30	1037.60	0.4 %
Natural gas	tcm	0.49	144.76	0.3 %

Note

bmt = billion metric tonnes; Bbbl = billion barrels; tcm = trillion cubic metres.

Source: British Petroleum 1997.

The indigenous production of commercial energy in India increased from 53 million tonnes of oil equivalent (mtoe) in 1972–73 to about 183mtoe in 1994–95, registering an average rate of growth of about 5.8 percent per annum (see Table 4.2). Given the large resources of coal, it is obvious that coal dominates the supply profile. However, while coal accounted for as much as 79 percent of domestically produced energy in 1972–73, its share declined to 69 percent in 1994–95. In direct contrast to this, the share of oil and gas increased from 16.3 percent to 27 percent in the same period. Table 4.2 gives the trend in the availability of primary energy forms.

Table 4.2

Availability of Primary Sources of Energy (mtoe)

	1972–73	1975–76	1980–81	1985–86	1990–91	1994–95
Coal						
Production	41.60	53.70	55.90	75.60	103.70	126.40
Net imports	0.25	0.23	0.68	0.89	2.40	4.00
Crude oil						
Production	7.30	8.40	10.50	30.20	33.00	32.20
Net imports	12.10	13.60	16.20	14.60	20.70	27.40
Natural gas						
Production	1.30	2.00	2.00	6.90	15.40	16.60
Net imports	—	—	—	—	—	—
Hydro power						
Production	2.30	2.80	3.90	4.30	6.00	7.00
Net imports	—	—	—	—	—	—
Nuclear power						
Production	0.09	0.22	0.25	0.42	0.52	0.48
Net imports	—	—	—	—	—	—
Total						
Production	52.59	67.12	72.55	117.42	158.62	182.68
Net imports	12.35	13.83	16.88	15.49	23.10	31.40

Source: TERI (1990) and (1997) including 10.7 mt of petroleum products.

Growing Oil Demand: Necessities and Concerns

On a per capita basis, India's consumption of commercial energy, at about 80 kilogram of oil equivalent (kgoe) per annum, was extremely low even in 1960–61. Despite these low levels of consumption, nearly 95 percent of oil consumption in 1960–61 was dependent on imports. In 1994, India's per capita energy consumption improved to 248kgoe per capita and its oil import dependence was at 65 percent.[1] When compared to the world average consumption of 1433kgoe per capita in 1994, Indian consumption levels are still abysmally low. The GOI recognizes the huge unsaturated demand for energy and hence the need to add enormous capacity. What are the choices that it has?

As highlighted earlier, despite large coal reserves, it is the share of oil and gas in total energy consumption that is increasing. The reasons for this are manifold, the most obvious being that the persistent shortages of coal and power supplies in the past have resulted in a switch to petroleum product consumption. This switch took place not as a result of the large supply of petroleum products available domestically, but of the relative ease in importing them.

The shortages of coal and electricity in the country arose largely due to inefficiencies, both in operations as well as in financial management of the producing entities. The energy sector in India was almost completely nationalized by the mid-1970s, and the government started using the sector as a vehicle for the provision of subsidies to its population as well as to provide employment. While on the one hand these sectors were straddled with employee numbers far beyond those required (and the accompanying labor problems), on the other hand they were never in a position to generate any substantial internal resources to augment the budgetary support provided by the government. Additionally, the subsidized energy provision resulted in scant regard being paid to energy efficiency by the consumers of energy as well. In short, demand growth always outstripped supply growth, which led to sub-optimal investment choices, and the spiral went on.

The fact that oil consumption continued to increase its share does not mean that the petroleum sector's performance was any better than that of the other energy sectors. Significant inefficiencies also exist in this sector, and large subsidies are provided on petroleum products as well. However, the Administered Pricing Mechanism (APM) designed for petroleum products, based on normative retention prices for ex-refinery products and a complex system of pool accounts numbering well over 100, ensured that while the oil pool account continued to increase its deficit, the public sector oil companies continued to remain cash rich. The failure of the petroleum sector is reflected in its inability to add significant new discoveries following Bombay High and in the fact that India is still a highly under-explored country.

The trends in reserves to production (R/P) ratios over the last 20 years for oil are exhibited in Figure 4.1. The R/P ratio for crude oil has remained largely the same during the latter part of the 1980s. While the ratio had gone up in the early 1990s due to planned containment of Bombay High production, it may not be possible to bring down the ratio in less than 20 to 25 years. Significant increases in oil production in the years to come, therefore, will depend upon the levels of reserve accretion.

With an acceleration in exploratory and developmental drilling, there was a substantial increase in the production of crude oil, at least until 1985–86. Production of crude oil rose from 6.8mt in 1970–71 to 33mt in 1990–91 but declined once again to 32.2mt in 1994–95 (see Table 4.3).

Figure 4.1

Reserves to Production (R/P) Ratios

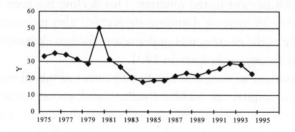

Note

Y represents the life of reserves in years.

Source: GOI, "Indian Petroleum and Natural Gas Statistics 1994–95" (New Delhi: Ministry of Petroleum and Natural Gas, 1996).

Table 4.3

Commodity Balance of Petroleum and Petroleum Products (mt)

	1970–71	1975–76	1980–81	1985–86	1990–91	1994–95[1]
Crude						
Domestic production	6.8	8.4	10.5	30.2	33.0	32.2
On-shore	6.8	8.4	5.5	9.4	11.8	12.0
Off-shore	—	—	5.0	20.8	21.2	20.2
Net imports	11.7	13.6	16.2	14.6	20.7	27.3
Refinery throughput	18.4	22.3	25.8	42.9	51.8	56.5
Petroleum products						
Domestic production	17.1	20.8	24.1	39.9	48.6	52.9
Light distillates	3.0	3.6	4.1	8.3	10.0	11.6
Middle distillates	8.6	10.8	12.1	21.6	26.4	28.7
Heavy ends	5.5	6.4	7.9	10.0	12.2	12.6
Net imports	0.8	2.0	7.3	1.9	6.1	10.7

Note

1 Provisional.

Source: GOI, "Indian Petroleum and Natural Gas Statistics, 1994–95" (New Delhi: Ministry of Petroleum and Natural Gas, 1996).

This increase has largely been due to an accelerated production from the Bombay High off-shore basin. In 1990–91, Bombay High accounted for 64 percent of crude oil produced in the country. However, as is already becoming obvious, production from Bombay High seems to have reached a plateau and may actually continue to decline.

Petroleum product consumption, which was growing at a rate of 5.7 percent over the 20 year period starting from 1970–71, has declined to a growth of 3.8 percent in the nineties. This decline has been largely due to an inability to increase domestic supply and also to increase imports substantially as the country was under severe foreign exchange stress, and was actually facing bankruptcy in 1991.

It is important to note that nearly 60 percent of the oil products consumed in the country are middle distillates and, correspondingly, almost all of the product imports are also of middle distillates. Amongst this category of products, the demand is almost entirely for kerosene and high speed diesel (HSD). These products, along with liquified petroleum gas (LPG) for the domestic sector and other products used by the fertilizer sector, have been under the APM, and have thus enjoyed significant subsidies.

Projected Hydrocarbons Demand/Supply Scenario

Tata Energy Research Institute (TERI) has estimated product demand (see Table 4.4). The total demand for major petroleum products is expected to reach a level of 189mt by the year 2011–12. These demands were estimated by undertaking a detailed analysis of the driving forces of demand for each product individually. This included looking at population demand projections, the rural/urban distribution, other socio-economic parameters, industry growth plans and projections for major industries, and special transport-related characteristics.

Table 4.4
Petroleum Product Demand Projections[1]

Product	1994–95	2001–02	2006–07	2011–12
LPG	3.43	7.44	11.54	16.66
Naphtha	3.40	7.18	11.68	18.90
Gasoline	4.14	7.35	11.57	16.23
Kerosene	8.96	13.10	15.70	18.51
High speed diesel	28.26	48.20	73.21	98.89
Fuel oil	9.89	13.91	17.50	19.80
Total[2]	58.08	97.18	141.20	188.99

Notes
1 Estimated by TERI.
2 Including minor products.

As such, it is expected that petroleum product demand in the coming years will grow at a little above seven percent over the period 1994–95 to 2011–12. This is a much higher growth rate than that experienced in the last two decades. Kerosene and HSD continue to account for a large share (55 percent) of total petroleum product consumption but the demand for light distillates is likely to grow very rapidly.

Even if we assume that 75 percent of the product demand would be met by domestic refineries – as is currently the case – domestic refineries would have to produce about 160mt of products. With refinery losses in India of 6.2 percent, this would translate into a refinery capacity requirement of approximately 170mt. In other words, India would require a near tripling of refinery capacity in the period until 2011–12 (refinery capacity in 1996–97 was slightly over 60mt) – a mere 15 years.

Looked at in terms of crude oil and taking into account ongoing efforts, oil production is likely to plateau at 40mt. India's self-sufficiency in crude oil will be down to less than 25 percent in 2011–12 apart from a product import requirement of 50mt. In 1995–96, India had a self sufficiency of 59 percent and product imports of less than 20mt.

Issues of Concern

The energy developments that have taken place in India over the last few decades have locked the country into a path of high oil dependence. Inadequate development of the coal sector, both in terms of mining capacity and transport infrastructure, and insufficient R&D attention to the development of clean coal technologies have placed limits on the extent that coal could be exploited for fulfilling India's energy needs. The strong voices emerging against the adverse environmental impacts of large hydropower development have already stymied the growth of this sector, while an unfocused R&D effort has failed to throw up viable, appropriate renewable energy technologies that could be utilized on a large scale.

At the same time, the rapid strides in crude oil production witnessed in the first half of the 1980s seem to have tapered off while demand continues to grow rapidly. The main issues that need urgent attention in this sector are:

- Inadequate exploration and production efforts leading to a fall in production and an inefficient pattern of exploitation;
- Poor financial flow situation in the entire industry due to mismanagement

of the pool accounts;

- High operational and cost inefficiencies across the industry brought about largely by the APM that reimburses on a cost-plus basis;
- Inadequate infrastructure availability, be it ports, refineries, pipelines, or other marketing infrastructure; and
- Increasing foreign exchange requirements accompanied by an increasing share of product imports vis-à-vis crude oil imports.

In addition, one needs to rationalize the production profile from the refineries to meet the growing demand for middle and light distillates. A suitable mix of imports of crude oil and petroleum products needs to be identified. In light of this, the expansion of current refineries and the establishment of new ones needs to be optimized to more closely match the demand profile.

Developments in the Hydrocarbons Industry

In 1990–91, India was faced with an enormous economic crisis that saw its gross fiscal deficit rise to 8.4 percent of GDP and a revenue deficit of 3.3 percent of GDP. The Gulf War added an unforeseen burden of US$2.9 billion to the current account and placed enormous pressure on India's already stressed foreign exchange reserves. At the end of June 1991, India barely had enough foreign currency reserves to finance two weeks of imports.

In response to this crisis, the GOI initiated a major economic reform program with the objectives of reducing deficits, improving foreign exchange reserves and accelerating GDP growth that had fallen to 1.2 percent in 1991–92. The broad based reform program included taxation revisions, devaluation of the rupee, liberalized trade policies, reduced governmental interference in industrial operations, and major restructuring of the power sector. The power sector reform program recognized both the poor financial status of the state electricity boards as well as the government's own inability to provide the enormous investments required to reduce the capacity shortage in this sector. Serious efforts were made to woo private investors into India's power generation activities and – given the country's poor investment credit rating – liberal incentives had to be provided for that purpose.

Recognizing the challenges posed by the petroleum sector, not least of which related to the need to wipe out the enormous deficits in the oil pool account, the GOI set up a Strategic Planning Group on Restructuring the Oil Industry in 1995 to outline a reforms' strategy for the hydrocarbons sector. The R Group, as it came to be called, was set up under the chairmanship of the Secretary, Ministry of Petroleum and Natural Gas (MoPNG) and consisted of representatives from both the public and private sector, economists, and other industry experts. This group, in its 1996 report, made several recommendations and also prepared a time-bound program for introducing reforms aimed at reducing the deficit in the oil pool account and encouraging the infusion of fresh capital into the sector. While it was recognized that competition and therefore greater efficiencies would follow new players, efficiency improvements were not a significant driving force for the reform program, of which the following is a summary.

Proposed Phasing of Reforms as Envisaged by the R Group

Phase I: 1996–98
- Rationalization of the retention margin;
- Withdrawal of the concept of a retention margin for refineries;
- Deregulation of natural gas pricing;
- Decanalization of furnace oil and bitumen;
- Partial deregulation of the marketing sector including freedom to appoint dealers and/or distributors; and
- Removal of the subsidy on HSD/reduction of the subsidy on kerosene, LPG, and input for fertilizer.

Phase II: 1998–2000
- Pricing of indigenous crude on the basis of average free on board (FOB) price of imported crudes (inclusive of cess and royalty);
- Rationalization of royalty and cess;
- Further deregulation of the marketing sector; and
- Further reduction of subsidy on kerosene, LPG, and input for fertilizers.

Phase III: 2000–02
- Decanalization of aviation turbine fuel, HSD, and mild steel (MS).

While the report was well received, some issues remain. First, the length of the transition period was considered by many to be too long. Second, the sequencing of reforms was considered unattractive by the industry. In particular, many would have preferred the marketing reforms in Phase I. Finally and most important, it was unclear when the reform process would be put in place.

While a political endorsement of the R Group report is still being debated, the MoPNG has implemented many of the report's recommendations. Recent developments have included a decision by the Union Cabinet to increase oil product prices. This decision involves dismantling the APM within two years as opposed to the five to six years proposed by the R Group. HSD prices increased by approximately 26 percent, bringing them in line with import parity prices, with the provision that prices be revised on a month to month basis, pegged to international prices. However, kerosene prices have not been altered while the subsidy on LPG continues, albeit at a lower level. The government has introduced a mechanism to help eradicate oil pool deficits, and it has announced plans to dismantle the APM.

In an attempt to open up the sector and increase private participation and investment, the government has introduced the following measures:

Upstream
- Bidding rounds offered for the exploration and production of hydrocarbons;
- Bidding for discovered oil and gas fields; and
- Bidding for speculative seismic surveys in sedimentary basins where seismic survey coverage is not adequate.

Downstream
- Parallel marketing by private parties of select products, namely LPG, kerosene, and low sulfur heavy stock; and
- The setting up of refineries in the joint and private sector.

The rationale behind the increased reliance on the private sector is driven by considerations of efficiency and increasing investment. Assuming a base case GDP growth of seven percent, a TERI report has estimated the investment demand by the energy sector to be US$476 billion, amounting to almost six percent of GDP.[2] Investments in the energy sector in India's Eighth Plan period (1992–97) were a mere two percent of GDP; in the future, government allocations would be reduced as they would be channeled more into social sectors. It is obvious, then, that private capital offers the only solution if a large scale energy crisis is to be avoided.

When the GOI allowed parallel marketing of kerosene and HSD by the private sector based on the decanalized imports of these products, opened up the lubricants market, and invited private companies to invest in the refineries sector, the response was tremendous, both from domestic and foreign companies. Most major multinational oil companies have reacted positively to these developments. Indeed the response to the government's initiative to set up new refineries may result in a glut of oil refining capacity. Thus, while the downstream market is likely to witness intense competition between domestic and foreign oil companies, it is estimated that the upstream market will see few new domestic players. Another major area of interest to foreign oil companies should be the shipping and port infrastructure associated with oil companies. Measures are afoot to open up this segment of the economy to private participation.

Outside Issues

One of the major demands of potential investors in India's refining sector has been the provision of an "effective" rate of protection. This essentially translates into a duty differential between that on crude oil imports and product imports; potential refiners have pegged this effective rate of protection at 20 to 25 percent. However, international experience says that a protection rate of between 5 percent and 10 percent would suffice to assure the economic attractiveness of domestically produced products over imported products. This issue is still under consideration by the ministry, and a decision should be taken shortly.

India needs to attract massive investments in refining and other related infrastructure sectors. As such, apart from the effective rate of protection, it may also have to offer the rights to market petroleum products in India as an incentive to those companies that have made significant investments in the oil infrastructure.

Other major concerns revolve around the concept of a "level playing field." Private parties have a real perception of threat from well established facilities and linkages of existing public sector undertakings, while the domestic public sector oil companies are concerned by the type of concessions made and the incentives provided to private and foreign oil companies in an effort to attract investments.

The GOI, in an effort to address these concerns, is attempting to separate itself from all operational issues. It is also in the process of defining the role and structure of regulatory bodies for the upstream and downstream oil sectors.

The regulatory framework will promote:

- The creation of a market based production, supply, distribution, and pricing system that promotes economic efficiency and competition. Such a system would provide products to consumers at a reasonable cost and lead to an optimal utilization of national resources;
- Ensuring energy security for the country and its citizens. This would translate into providing consumers with adequate and secure supplies of products at all times; and
- Environmental protection. Ensuring that the industry operates under principles that recognize the importance of protecting the environment and mitigate any kind of damage that resource extraction, transportation, and utilization have on the environment.

The ministry's responsibility would then be focused on setting policies for the oil sector, i.e., defining the rules under which companies will operate in the Indian oil sector. For example, these rules would pertain to downstream issues such as announcing the timing and sequencing of deregulation, or determining the need, extent, and time period over which tariff protection would be extended to oil refineries.

The regulatory body would ensure that:

- Rules laid down by the MoPNG are adhered to;
- Entry to the market is not restricted;
- Industry does not indulge in cartelization; and
- Above all, consumer interests are safeguarded.

Conclusion

The Indian oil sector is at an exciting stage of designing and implementing a variety of reforms. Moreover, these reforms will undoubtedly have an impact on the oil producing countries of the Middle East. Areas which will be affected include:

- Investment opportunities in both exploration and production activities as well as refining and other downstream activities in India;
- A change in the balance between crude oil import requirements and product import requirements in India towards a larger percentage of crude imports to feed new refineries. This may have implications for decisions on establishing refining capacity in those countries that consider India a major market for petroleum products;
- As the likelihood of adopting international standards for both

operational and environmental parameters is high, this may have an implication for the sourcing of crude and products itself; and
• The entry of a large number of multinational oil companies, with their backward linkages, may have implications for state oil companies in the Middle East.

The Indian oil experience is interesting in that it offers an insight into issues resulting from excessive governmental intervention, provision of perverse subsidies, inadequate diversification of both supply and demand of energy products, and gross financial mismanagement.

CHAPTER 5

Issues in Deregulation, Privatization, and Reregulation of the Energy Industries

Paul Horsnell

Introduction

This chapter covers an agenda of issues that relate to structural change and, in the loosest sense, liberalization of energy. In particular, it concentrates on the oil industry with reference to the oil sectors of the Gulf exporters. It should be noted that the merits of the various forms of liberalization in oil have developed far later than in other energy industries and in the utilities. This is due to the nature of the commodity, and to historical accidents and coincidences.

The general move towards the policy implications of the school of economic thought broadly defined as "new classicism" or the "new economic orthodoxy" began with theoretical developments over the course of the 1960s and 1970s. In macroeconomics, the work of Robert Lucas[1] *inter alia* began to redefine the role of state as well as the nature and importance of private expectations. In microeconomics, the role of incentives and information began to be stressed more through developments such as principal agent and contract theory. The older Keynesian view of benign interventionist governments began to lose currency, and politically there was the rise of economically radical parties of the right in the developed world.

This was where history intervened. The first oil shock had the parallel impact of making general economic policy more liberal, while making policy towards oil far more interventionist. At the policy level, through the general macroeconomic turbulence, it hastened the demise of the Keynesian view of government, and reinforced the practical willingness to turn to more radical liberal policies. For oil, it heightened the perception that oil was too strategic a commodity to be left to the market. Policy became dominated by supply security and resource nationalism, with general economic and foreign affairs concerns driving far greater interventionism.

The move back from this position in oil has been slow and often uncertain. It should be noted that the recent measures that have been taken as pure economic liberalization in many countries, both producing and consuming, have in fact gone little further than to restore the pre-1973 status quo. This is true of the US, and also of most Asian oil sectors now going through liberalization processes. A glance through the list of current state oil companies, both upstream and downstream, reveals that most were created or took their current form in the 1970s. Liberalization in other sectors has involved dismantling the structures created by economic views of state intervention; in oil, most of those structures arose at a different time and for very different purposes.

Downstream there are strategic considerations; upstream there is the overwhelming impact of the presence of rent. In contrast, electricity liberalization involves changes to vertically integrated structures with a dominating presence of natural monopoly in transmission. The rent issues are all associated with that monopoly, just as they are for gas, water, railways, and (in the case of local networks) telecommunications. In oil, natural monopoly considerations are less important, and the rent is a genuine resource rent rather than a transmission rent.

Beyond changes in general economic outlook, the question of oil industry structure has started to become an issue in Gulf countries due to developments specific to the oil market. First, particularly since 1993, non-OPEC production has increased significantly, alongside a reduction in the cost function and an expansion of the ability to stretch out limited reserve bases. For example, the rise of Norway to the rank of second largest oil exporter in the world, well in excess of Kuwait, the UAE, and Iran, brings to the fore the issue of precisely when Gulf members of OPEC will be able to garner the bulk of incremental world oil demand. Second, there is the impact of the reorganization of the industry in some OPEC member countries, often accompanied by a tendency for those countries to operate outside of the OPEC core. In particular, the Venezuelan *apertura* represents a challenge, given the ambitious production expansion plans and the movement of immense sums from foreign capital markets into the Venezuelan industry. In the longer-term, the opening up of the Iraqi industry, with a wave of French, Russian, and Chinese capital already poised, raises further questions. The third main factor relates to changes within Gulf companies, and in particular the emergence of a younger generation of skilled technocrats who, given their training and historical context, can be said to see oil operations as more of an economic operation rather than a political one, unlike the previous cohorts of company administrators and planners.

Changes in the industry are all too often wrapped up in the single catch-all concept of "liberalization," each strand of reform akin to one of the Hydra's heads. The term is not that useful, given that it is used to cover a range of potential options. These include privatization of a state company, commercialization of the company within the state framework, the dismantlement of monopoly and the entry of foreign capital, and changes in the regulatory or fiscal regimes. Two parties can engage in a discussion on oil industry liberalization only to discover that they are working with two mutually exclusive definitions of what liberalization actually entails. The components of possible liberalization raise very different issues, and the answer for any given country's structure need not involve all, or even any, of those possibilities.

Liberalization, of whatever form, does not mean that the role of government subsides, merely that it takes on different forms and works through different structures. The reregulation of the oil industry is the process whereby those new mechanisms exert themselves. This is where oil differs from the industries normally in the vanguard of liberalization, i.e., electricity and telecommunications. By dint of the sheer size and international nature of oil, it has both economic and political strategic implications which dictate that the state is extremely unlikely to leave itself without a considerable array of control mechanisms. For example, the US oil industry is, in economic terms, highly liberal. Yet it would be naive to believe that the US government does not exert a considerable degree of control over the oil market. Control can be exerted through foreign policy actions, regulatory agencies and controls, the use of strategic stocks, fiscal policy both downstream and upstream, direct mandate, environmental policy and legislation, and straightforward persuasion. I will briefly deal with the forms that reregulation has taken, with particular reference to the use of environmental legislation, later in the chapter.

In vertically integrated utilities, the UK is often put forward as having provided a series of templates for liberalization. The final section shows that there was no template for oil. Indeed, a government that could be accommodatory and liberal in other industries, and attempt to base its policy on firm microeconomic foundations, had no such base when it came to oil. Its attitude to foreign capital tends to show that even an economically radical government still resorted to a form of resource nationalism.

The UK Experiment and the Oil Sector

The effects of the policies laid down by the three Thatcher governments in the UK between 1979 and 1990 have been well documented elsewhere.[2] In terms of the model it laid down, the policy can be divided into two main facets. The first was the reliance on market solutions wherever possible, and elsewhere on the creation of quasi-markets. All transactions, including internal transactions within state institutions, were ideally to be conducted through some form of market at a market price. The second facet was a redefinition of the role of the state, with a large scale transference from the public to the private sector. It should be noted that, in the context of the UK, the program was not primarily one of stripping away layers of regulation, but rather one of imposing regulation in cases where the market solution was deemed to be sub-optimal. The four largest privatizations (telecommunications, electricity, water, and gas) all involved vertically integrated operations with a natural monopoly at the transmission stage. The program and its effects came down in the end to choices of how to balance between structural solutions and price regulation. As such, however influential in the demonstration of the general principles of reform, the program encompassed issues which are not directly relevant to the deregulation of oil. The importance of the experiment in this regard lay more in the general statement of the state's role and the demonstration of the possible scale of the efficiency gains achievable under the new structures, as well as the potential for fiscal accumulation.

The UK experiment did not encompass any major reform of the oil industry, and its application to the sector was minor. It is true that the UK did in effect have two national oil companies, but these did not fit the general structure of such companies in other countries. One of the national oil companies, *de facto*, was BP through the government's majority share holding, but the company was never really an instrument of central control or policy. The holding in BP did not date from the economic consensus of the wartime coalition government, which was reflected in the nationalization of key industries by the socialist government that came to power in 1945. Government involvement thus did not stem from the desire to use industry for macroeconomic or social justice targets, and in the main tended to be thought of as a national equity asset rather than as part of the public sector.[3] The government's majority share was purchased in 1914 (one of the earliest government interventions in industry), and stemmed primarily from a desire to attain security of supply for naval needs, as well as preserving the independence of the then Anglo-Persian Oil Company. The proponent of the bill to buy the stake was Winston Churchill, who represented it as an astute investment rather than as an act of interventionism.[4] Direct guidelines on the nature of the one step removed relationship between government and company were written into the original agreement and, to the greatest extent, followed. Policy towards BP was one of the easier decisions for the new Thatcher government. It was already commercialized, and already had a stock market listing. The only question was the mechanism of sale and a calculation as to how much stock the market could absorb at once. A first tranche of the BP holding was sold quickly, with a second tranche sold in 1987, leaving only a minor government share in the company.

However, it should be noted that the government proved to be less than *laissez-faire* with respect to foreign capital when Kuwait built up its holdings in BP. After a Monopolies and Mergers Commission report, it was decided that the size of Kuwait's shareholding was not in the public interest. The solution forced onto the parties was one which not only demonstrated that the belief in the solutions provided by equity markets was less than total, it also laid the foundation for BP's later period of financial distress. While BP recovered, the verdict on government intervention can still only be considered as negative. Given the general thrust of the government's economic policy, it is ironic that the episode was one of the two most direct government interventions into BP over the then 70-year history of its relationship with the government.

The other national oil company in the UK was the British National Oil Corporation (BNOC), which is slightly more identifiable as such in the international context. Founded in 1975, BNOC had two main functions. First, it was a direct participant in upstream activity. Second, it received royalty payments in oil on behalf of the government, and thus (there being no government-owned refineries) had a trading role in disposing of the royalty crude. BNOC proved to be short-lived. The upstream interests were privatized in 1982 as Britoil, and the bulk of the company was dissolved in 1985. As has been argued by Mabro et al., BNOC was never really allowed to become an effective national oil company.[5] It had a trading role, yet was denied the infrastructure and, in particular, storage necessary for trading. In a country moving to market price solutions, BNOC was left to use an often politically directed price structure, which left it at a considerable disadvantage to commercial operations.

In short, oil was being treated differently to other sectors of the economy. The policy choices regarding BNOC were either to allow it to become an effective national oil company in its own right, or to simply abandon it. The flotation of Britoil removed the first option; in reality, it would have been less distortionary to have abolished BNOC immediately afterwards. However inefficient the mechanism, and however insufficient the tools the BNOC traders had at their disposal, the overall effect was that the UK government was providing an administered oil price. Arguably, this was not only distorting the UK oil market, usually to the direct loss of the tax payer, it was also a destabilizing force in the international market.

The UK government also divested itself of its other upstream oil interests. The oil production holdings of the then nationalized British Gas were separated in 1982 and floated off as Enterprise Oil, now a successful international upstream company. The rest of British Gas followed Enterprise into the private sector in 1986. Overall there was really no grand strategy for the oil industry in the program, other than the straightforward desire to move it all out of the state sector. Indeed, as in the case of intervention in BP and the role of BNOC up to 1985, oil seems to have been treated differently in relation to other industries in that the effect of oil policies was running behind the criteria and instruments being used in other industries.

The UK experiment was primarily about ownership. Regulation was considerably increased as a result of the process, as the new industrial forms contained elements of natural monopoly and integrated structures that would not, left alone, produce competitive market solutions. In contrast, liberalization in the oil industry is primarily concerned with removing existing layers of regulation. Except perhaps in the case of oil pipelines, natural monopoly aspects are almost absent. As a result, the privatization of oil assets does not normally imply the need for the creation of new regulatory structures if there are no barriers to entry. In short, beyond very general economic principles, the UK experiment carried very little direct information for a country seeking to promote oil liberalization. Indeed, to some extent, elements of the information it carried could be construed as distinctly unhelpful, for example the view of foreign capital implicit in the Kuwait and BP affair.[6]

The Facets of Liberalization

PRIVATIZATION

Privatization of oil is perhaps the most emotive component of any potential liberalization, involving as it does issues of resource nationalism and also large scale income distribution. It is worth noting that the theoretical justification for privatization in a general application is in fact not completely clear cut. The components of conventional economic wisdom have been cogently described by Laffont and Tirole, who see five main constituents in the arguments for privatization.[7] First, state companies suffer from an absence of capital market monitoring. Second, they have a soft budget constraint which encourages inefficiency. Third, they suffer from expropriation of investments by the state, which also impacts on managerial incentives and efficiency. Fourth, there is a lack of precise objectives, created in large part by multiplicity and impermanence in government policy. Fifth, governments are subject to lobbying activity and pressure from interest groups to direct welfare enhancing activities of state enterprises in their direction.

As Laffont and Tirole point out, these are not always straightforward or complete arguments. The first, for instance, does not help to distinguish between full and partial privatizations, and is not of much use as a justification when the domestic capital market is ossified or simply inefficient. When the choice is between a state enterprise and a private regulated enterprise, the four and fifth reason would apply just as much to the privatized firm. The third reason is incomplete, and needs a further argument to explain why the problem does not also occur when the controllers are shareholders rather than government.

Therefore, the five conventional wisdom justifications do not bear close scrutiny. Indeed, of those five, Laffont and Tirole again advance the theory that there are just two primary differences between public and private firms. First, even partial public ownership reduces the incentives for acquisition of information by the capital market, resulting in a share price that is not a good measure of managerial performance. Rephrased, this means that private capital is less interested in companies that have even residual state ownership. The degree of state ownership that causes this effect to be a major problem is difficult to specify. However, interest could be expected to wane sharply when that residual ownership is actually a majority share. In terms of capital market incentives, it is doubtful that government shares below 50 percent would represent major distortionary effects. However, the argument is that more partial privatizations produce few discernible improvements in managerial incentives and efficiency, and thus little improvement in company performance. The second argument is that the objectives of state and private ownership may differ in ways that do impact significantly on economic outcomes.

The result of the above is that private versus public ownership comes down to the balance of two effects. Privatization is beneficial because private managers invest more (and in more rational ways) than do state managers, as they (and the company) are more likely to benefit from those investments. The trade-off comes only if the private firm is regulated, in which case negative effects on cost efficiency arise from the conflict of interest between regulator and shareholder. Note that, compared to utilities with a natural monopoly transmission stage, the degree of operational regulation post privatization that many (but not all) state oil companies face is relatively light.

In total, the theory is that the benefits of privatization come through investment, but only if the privatization is not partial. This raises two problems for the case of oil. First, flotation of even partial portions of a state oil company can pose considerable capital market absorption problems, i.e., greater than 50 percent flotations can be logistically impossible even if politically acceptable. Most of the world's major state oil companies in exporting companies are extremely large relative to their domestic capital market. To give but one example, as of 1997 the estimated value of Petróleos de Venezuela (PDVSA) under conventional accounting is some five times the size of the total valuation of capitalized Venezuelan companies. Market capitalization across the whole of Latin America is large, some 5 percent of the world total, but PDVSA would be about 15 percent of that entire regional capitalization. In absorption terms, companies such as Saudi Aramco, KPC, and ADNOC are even larger in terms of current national and regional capitalizations. Flotations would then have to be either extremely small scale (and therefore bring few benefits), or centered heavily on international capital markets, or both. In short, for capital market reasons alone, even disregarding the broader political and economic consequences, privatization is not as yet a meaningful option.

The second problem concerns investment. If the benefit of privatization operates mainly through more and better investment, then there is no benefit if the level of investment is voluntarily constrained. This leads to the striking conclusion that as long as Saudi Arabia, Kuwait, and Abu

Dhabi maintain a policy within OPEC of voluntarily restraining output, and also have no problems in maintaining the desired extent of spare capacity, then privatization of Saudi Aramco, KPC, or ADNOC would produce no economic benefits, even if the capital market problems could be overcome. The scope for privatization is then fairly limited, and indeed is confined to subsidiary or margin activities of the companies and not to the vast bulk of their activities.

One could also note that there is a social trade-off involved in the Gulf that is more important than in other countries. Privatization is often justified in terms of seeking greater efficiency. That can be achieved in other, better ways, such as commercialization, discussed in the next subsection. However, the most direct and easiest way for a privatized company to realize efficiencies is through labor shedding. Given the scale of labor shedding achieved in the last decade by major oil companies and also by some Latin American national oil companies, it would be difficult to sustain the argument that Gulf national oil companies were completely lean in their use of labor. There would clearly be scope for some considerable reduction in the workforce. However, in economies where graduate and skilled unemployment is a social problem, a policy that greatly exacerbates the employment problem carries a potentially immense social cost. Under those circumstances, a policy that removed the ability of national oil companies to absorb a significant portion of the graduate labor pool is unlikely to represent a rational course of action. Before the rest of the economic structure has built up that absorption capacity, efficiency savings through oil company redundancies is in all likelihood both economically and politically unviable.

COMMERCIALIZATION

The alternative to full or partial privatization can be loosely described as commercialization, i.e., the process whereby a state company attempts to proxy the behavior of a private company. The most developed example of this is perhaps the Norwegian state oil company, Statoil, where the company acts as an internationalized upstream and downstream company in competition, and sometimes cooperation, with international oil majors in both domestic and foreign operations.

Full commercialization involves a series of measures. These include the implementation of full transfer pricing within the company, the ability to seek funds on the international capital market in the company's own name, full accounting within each subdivision of the company, the end of cross-subsidization between activities, and pricing structures that proxy world prices or, where relevant, opportunity costs, in all the company's activities. Benchmarking can provide an alternative to the information effects of having a share price. As a further attempt to proxy capital market behavior, Statoil even commissions external auditors to value the company to provide a measure of the year-to-year changes in the capitalization proxy for the company. However, the most important set of measures towards full commercialization are in the company's relationship with the government. In short, that relationship needs to be extremely well defined. In particular, commercialization and the provision of full incentives is not possible when the government sees the company and its investment funds as an extension of the Treasury. Commercialization effectively involves the agreement of a tax structure in advance, so that the company's obligations to the government are well defined. It is imperative that the government does not seek to use the state company for objectives outside of the oil sector (e.g., as a labor market sponge or as a mechanism for income redistribution); this is extremely difficult in economies dominated by the oil sector.

It might also be noted that in some circumstances, commercialization (and internationalization) of a company can arise if the relationship with government is badly defined. For example, PDVSA's commercialization and internationalization can both be seen as defensive reactions to a weak and, in terms of the demands on PDVSA's capital funds in the past, often perfidious political system.[8]

In terms of the Gulf state oil companies, elements of commercialization are possible and, indeed, have been implemented. Many structural and managerial changes have been incorporated in order to remove dead weight losses. Management is as professional as in a commercialized company, and the bulk of decisions are made on strictly commercial grounds. There has been significant internationalization in the down-stream. In the upstream, internationalization has only been achieved outside the Gulf by the highly commercialized state companies of Norway and Malaysia (Statoil and Petronas), and for other reasons by the rather uncommercialized Chinese National Petroleum Corporation. However, given the scale of the Gulf industry relative to the rest of the economy and the political realities of operation, full commercialization does not as yet represent a viable way forward.

Breaking the Monopoly: Allowing the Entry of Foreign Capital

This is one of the few areas where the structure of Gulf oil industries differ. Foreign capital plays an upstream role in the UAE, Qatar, Oman, Yemen, and now Iraq, while it is still absent in Kuwait and Saudi Arabia. Indeed, beyond the latter two countries, Mexico is now the only other significant producing country where foreign capital is not used to explore for and develop oil. The list of countries barring foreign capital was until recently much longer, but since the start of the 1980s among significant producers, there has been an opening up in China, Russia, Azerbaijan, Kazakhstan, Algeria, Iran, Iraq, Venezuela, and Vietnam (albeit in some cases only partially).

There are numerous conditions under which an opening to foreign capital is rational, but it should be noted in advance that none of the following list of conditions currently applies to either Kuwait or Saudi Arabia. Foreign involvement can help if the state oil company either faces capital, managerial, or technology constraints, or is unable to absorb the full extent of geological risk and develop the more challenging prospects. While the constraints accepted as part of OPEC membership are binding, the opening up of the upstream is unlikely to force its way to the top of the agenda.

In the context of the latter point, it is precisely because the constraints of OPEC membership are no longer accepted that Venezuela and Iraq have opened up. The Venezuelan *apertura* and the likely future behavior of Iraq represent significant threats to the core Gulf OPEC countries. The argument runs as follows. For several years, Gulf OPEC members have only received a small portion of incremental world oil demand. While demand has been, and remains, extremely strong, non-OPEC has surged. This has happened with global oil capital mainly confined to exploration in high cost frontier areas such as the North Sea and the deepwater US Gulf of Mexico. With that capital now gaining access to more prospective and lower cost areas, while maintaining the cost reductions and technological improvements gained in response to the years of low prices and high cost frontier exploration, the potential barrel increment per dollar of international capital invested is increasing.

This gives rise to the only scenario in which serious consideration could be given to the opening up of Saudi Arabia and Kuwait. The capital pool for non-core OPEC development was not dried up by the 1986 price fall, due to the degree of cost savings achievable and due to accommodatory fiscal changes in non-OPEC areas. If that capital pool is considered limited, then allowing foreign capital in reduces the capital available for other parts of the world. In other words, if the slack in the market does not exist for Saudi Arabia to produce the incremental barrel itself, then it is better for that barrel to be produced in Saudi Arabia by a foreign company than it is for it to be produced by the same company elsewhere. This comes down to a judgment about the elasticity of the capital market, and of the technical and managerial constraints in foreign companies. If the supply of capital is perfectly elastic, and if the development of Saudi operations does not impact on the capability of a major oil company to maintain or wish to maintain all its existing exploration and development projects in more marginal areas, then the argument fails.

Reducing Direct Regulation

A further facet of liberalization is changes in the degree or nature of direct government regulation. This tends to be more of a feature of the downstream of consuming countries, but does have some application to the Gulf. There are eleven main forms of direct regulation, ten of which are listed below, with the eleventh being considered in the context of reregulation in the final section:[9]

- Government controls on entry or the maintenance of statutory monopolies;
- Constraints on the movement of foreign capital;
- Direct price or quantity controls;
- Minimum inventory constraints;
- Constraints on construction;
- Constraints on integration;
- Constraints on national oil company investment;
- Import and export restrictions. Governments may ban imports or exports of certain products, or place restrictions and conditions on importers. Import bans are motivated by balance of payment and foreign exchange considerations, as well as being protectionist towards the domestic refining industry. Export constraints are more likely to be motivated by supply security concerns, or occasionally, as in the case of Alaskan oil, have an element of protectionism towards some part of the labor force such as seamen. In some cases, where logistics imply that a country will have both imports and exports of the same product, an export ban can be little more than an indirect import ban.

Such controls may also be tariff rather than quota based (e.g., discriminatory tariffs on imported crude oil or oil products). A further form of insulation for domestic producers can arise in the form of differential tariffs for inputs and outputs. For instance, a regime where oil product imports carry a higher tariff than crude oil, provides a form of protectionism for domestic oil refiners. Indeed, if a government feels that, due to the operation of other considerations of national costs and benefits, a degree of protection is justified, then the differential import tariff often provides a highly efficient method for achieving this;[10]

- Rate of return regulation; and
- Foreign exchange constraints. Particularly in countries which operate systems of dual or multi-tier exchange rates, companies may be forced to conduct different operations at different rates, usually to their disadvantage. Alternatively, a national company may be rationed not just in its access to capital, but specifically in the amount of foreign exchange it can utilize. One final form of this constraint is the imposition of limitations on the amount of profit earned by foreign capital that can be repatriated.[11]

This list represents a daunting array of instruments that a government can use to affect outcomes in the oil industry. It is worth noting that the often used argument for liberalization in the Gulf oil sector, i.e., that everywhere else has liberalized, is something of a red herring. Even in developed and, in economic terms, liberal economies, the degree of regulation over oil, utilizing varying components of the list, is often highly significant. In terms of the Gulf countries, many of the potential liberalizations from those elements of the above taxonomy that currently bind only become possible within the context of general capital market development and trade liberalization. Some, such as the setting (and sometimes enforcement) of domestic oil product and electricity prices involve broader considerations of equity and income distribution; others are wrapped up in the question of creating clearer dividing lines between the roles of government and state oil companies.

The Reregulation of Oil

Liberalization in oil is perhaps better defined as a process whereby the governments' control mechanisms over the industry alter, rather than one whereby government control disappears. In consuming countries, concerns of supply security, the use of oil as a macroeconomic control mechanism, and the attraction of the sector as a source of large, and in real terms ever increasing, downstream taxation receipts. Through taxation, governments affect relative fuel prices. Through other policy areas, most notably in transport, impact on oil's share in the energy mix. In short, the panoply of control mechanisms remains extremely large.

To illustrate, here is just one aspect of the reregulation of oil, namely the use of environmental specifications for oil products in ways that are not always purely driven by environmental concerns. The Asian market provides a good example where the environmental specifications for gasoline and most especially gasoil have in recent years been tightened at a severe rate. In many cases, it is clear that, having lifted direct controls on differential crude oil and oil product import tariffs, requiring a very difficult or unusual product specification is seen as a way of reintroducing some form of protection for domestic oil refiners. For example, in Japan the price of gasoline has been depressed by liberalization that effectively forced Japanese prices to adjust closer to the border price of Korean gasoline. Pressure has therefore grown for the adoption of tighter standards, such as sub-one percent benzene content. Such a specification is beyond the capability of the Korean industry to produce in significant quantities, and would immediately begin to force domestic prices up away from the border price.

As a subsidiary benefit in the eyes of government, tightening sulfur specifications on gasoil is also a mechanism for impacting on trade flows. In particular, it forces refiners to choose between the capital cost of refinery upgrading, or paying the premium for obtaining additional low sulphur crude oil. Given the differentials that were obtained over most of the 1990s, in most cases the most cost effective solution has been substitution in the crude oil slate run by refiners. The significance of this is that it has increased the relative demand for oil in Asia from Abu Dhabi, Oman, Yemen, West Africa, and even the North Sea, and tended to reduce the relative incremental demand for Iranian, Kuwaiti, and the bulk of Saudi oil. Taiwan now has a term contract with Norway. Such flows are mainly due to the fact that the location of most incremental crude oil supply in recent years has been in the Atlantic basin, while the location of most incremental demand has been in Asia. However, the flows are also a direct consequence of the tightening of environmental specifications.

A further example of reregulation is provided by China. Having to a great extent liberalized oil flows and promoted a strong element of competition between state oil companies, there has been a major retrenchment in policy and reregulation of oil since 1994. Oil has become the easiest mechanism of macroeconomic control. When faced with an inflationary surge, with monetary policy ineffective, the bulk of fiscal policy delegated to the provinces, and the dismantlement of the system of central allocation, it proved most effective to re-license oil imports and bring down economic growth and inflation by in effect rationing the flow of oil to industry. In the case of oil, government then rarely goes away.

CHAPTER 6

Electricity Privatization in England and Wales: A Case Study

Gordon MacKerron

Introduction

Privatization of the electricity supply industry in England and Wales has been much studied and imitated. Countries as diverse as Colombia and Ukraine have been advised to follow important elements of the English model and some have made real attempts to follow the advice. This chapter outlines some distinctive features of English privatization,[1] and suggests lessons that might be learned by countries contemplating their own privatization process.[2] While many lessons can be learned, it is suggested that any direct copying of the English experience is unlikely to be appropriate.

The Constituent Parts of Privatization

There are a number of terms – often used loosely and sometimes interchangeably – that deserve some definition. These include privatization, liberalization, and deregulation. There are other terms, such as restructuring, and vertical or horizontal deintegration that also need to be placed in context.[3] Below is an attempt to unpick the various strands within the wider process of "privatization."

CORPORATIZATION
This is a term used to describe a process – particularly necessary in some developing and transition economies – of transforming utility activities from an arm of Government (the Ministry of Electric Power) to a corporate structure. In other words, the electricity supply industry must

first be changed from a part of the civil service into something that is recognizably constituted and run as a business, using the managerial structure and accounting methods of the private corporation.

PRIVATIZATION

This appears to be the least problematic idea, as it seems simply to express the change in ownership from public to private. In practice, however, some governments use the term "privatization" when they mean little more than corporatization. In some of the apparently privatized electricity companies, for instance in Southeast Asia, governments continue to hold a large majority of the shares. Thus the degree of privatization varies substantially between countries and over time. In the electricity sector particularly, governments often wish to retain majority or minority share holdings, and may choose to keep control over strategic parts of the industry, especially the high voltage network. However, labeling this process "privatization" is not very helpful.

LIBERALIZATION

This is a very general idea, but is normally taken to mean a process in which trade restrictions are reduced (they are rarely abolished in electricity), and discriminatory or subsidized arrangements are removed. This may or may not have any direct connection with the process of privatization. The classic act of liberalization in the electricity supply industry (ESI) is the establishment of "third party access." This means allowing improved and preferably equal access to the high voltage network for all potential generators, in contrast to the traditional position where a single generating utility has sole rights of access to transport, or at best imposes discriminatory conditions on other potential users of the system. An important step towards liberalization in Europe is the 1996 Electricity Directive of the European Union, introducing the possibility of large customers choosing their electricity supplier. This can be implemented irrespective of the ownership status of European utilities.

RESTRUCTURING AND DEINTEGRATION

Although restructuring is a loose term, in the context of the ESI the most common meaning is the attempt to deintegrate the industry vertically. This involves separating out some or all of the sequential stages of the industry: generation (production of electricity), transmission (high voltage transport), distribution (low voltage transport), and retail supply. The critical deintegration activity is the separation of the transmission system from control of the incumbent and usually monopolistic generator. This opens the possibility of "third party access" on equal terms to all potential generators, and thus is designed to stimulate competitive behavior, either in generation or (less commonly) in retail supply. Competition in generation can either be full-scale (e.g., breaking the generating part of the industry into several companies or "horizontal" deintegration) or incremental, by allowing new private capital to invest in new plants and sell through the opened-up transmission system by a variety of institutional devices.

DEREGULATION

This is the final – and easily the most misleading – idea. The idea of deregulation is sometimes advocated by those who believe, in some cases quite reasonably, that the state has had a negative and sometimes arbitrary impact on the evolution of the industry. However, successful deregulation – "leaving it to the market" – requires a high level of effective competition between a significant number of operators, and the absence of natural monopoly characteristics.[4] It also helps if the market being deregulated is for a non-strategic commodity of low political significance. It is evident that electricity fits none of these categories. There has rarely been much effective competition in electricity (except in supplying large industrial consumers and possibly in bidding for new generating capacity); the wires business is a large natural monopoly; and electricity is politically and strategically vital. The real challenge in privatization is therefore effective reregulation, often involving new state agencies at arm's length from traditional Ministries of Energy.

The UK "Big Bang" Approach to Privatization

In the UK, privatizations have tended to be large, all-embracing events, with all the major characteristics of the relevant industry changing simultaneously. In electricity, virtually all of the ideas spelled out above were introduced, and mostly at a single date in 1990. Corporatization had clearly taken place some years in advance of privatization, but in 1990 an

attempt was made simultaneously to:
- Implement vertical deintegration;
- Introduce competition in generation and supply;
- Start up a new wholesale trading mechanism;
- Reregulate through a new regulatory body; and
- Transfer ownership to the private sector.

More specifically, in England in April 1990 a large number of changes took place at the same time:
- Three new companies generating electricity were created out of the single monopoly generator/transmitter, the Central Electricity Generating Board (CEGB) (though within the CEGB, the new companies had been engaged in "shadow trading" for about a year before they were legally constituted or "vested");
- A new National Grid Company was also created out of the old CEGB, to be responsible for high voltage transmission;
- The distribution companies were allowed to generate up to 15 percent of their needs, and had their monopoly of retail sales to large consumers ended;
- A new electricity trading system, the Pool, was created, to act both as a day-ahead market for wholesale transactions, and to allow a new form of merit order dispatch to be created based on price bids from generators; and
- A new agency, the Office of Electricity Regulation (OFFER) was created with wide powers to regulate the monopoly elements of the industry, and to foster competition in the generation and retail supply sectors.[5]

The underlying idea of these changes was that competition would, wherever possible, become the new organizing principle of the industry. This was liberalization on a large scale, though there was little attempt to claim that there would be serious deregulation – the most optimistic view was that deregulation was a long-term ambition.[6]

The actual sale of the new companies took a few months because even a relatively large and sophisticated capital market like London could not easily absorb the very large asset transfer of the English electricity supply industry (some US$15 billion in all) in a simultaneous set of transactions. Nevertheless, a huge change in the nature of the system was effected more or less overnight.

This "big bang" approach to privatization appears to have two main roots. The first is the fact that the primary motivation of this privatization, as with all the other major British privatizations, was to raise cash for the public sector.[7] Objectives of efficiency, competition, and wider share ownership were present and of real importance, but it is impossible to imagine that the huge upheavals in British economic structures in the ten years after 1983 would have occurred without the public sector financial motive. During the late 1980s, the British Treasury became virtually dependent on receiving some US$8 billion annually from privatizations, and used the money either to reduce taxes or minimize borrowing. This was achieved by privatizing large sectors of publicly-owned assets one by one on a virtually annual basis. A longer drawn out event, with revenue appearing over several years, would have made public sector financial planning much more difficult and would have postponed the much-desired receipt of sale proceeds into the Treasury.

The second root of the "big bang" was that large and simultaneous changes were possible in British circumstances. The electricity industry was not in crisis, and was in many respects quite successful. There was certainly room for much improvement in the old state-owned system, especially in planning and investment strategy, but the system was operationally efficient, was experiencing virtually zero demand growth, and had surplus capacity in generation and the network. It therefore suffered from no serious structural problems. The industry was also financially in good shape – almost free of debt and earning an annual operating surplus of around UK£1 billion.[8] In such unproblematic circumstances, it was relatively easy to experiment, and to introduce quite radical organizational change. Few other countries, and virtually none outside the OECD, are so free of major structural or financial problems in their ESIs as they approach the issue of privatization.

The Regulation of Monopoly

While competition was to be the major feature of the new system, there were elements of natural monopoly that were to remain indefinitely. These were the transmission business of National Grid (high voltage), and the distribution businesses of the distribution companies (low voltage wires). In addition, retail supply to customers in the household sector was to remain a monopoly for eight years.

The rate of return approach to natural monopoly regulation, typical of practices in the US, was rejected in the UK in favor of a price cap control.

In this new system, prices charged for the use of the natural monopoly systems had to be transparent, and could only rise by less than the general annual level of inflation. This is the "RPI minus x" system in which x is meant to reflect efficiency gains achievable by the regulated monopolists.[9] Again, unlike the US system, price cap reviews were scheduled for every four to five years, rather than in the annual cycle used in the US. The main reason for these longer periods was to allow longer-term planning for the regulated companies and to ease regulatory burdens.

The intention was to make regulation as light and simple as possible, and to minimize information required by OFFER. Experience has been somewhat different.[10] The initial price caps, especially for the distributors, were set mostly by the government and were much too lenient. For five years, the distribution companies were subject to RPI plus x. In other words, the distributors could charge higher real prices for the use of the distribution network over five years. This made the distribution companies enormously profitable over the 1990–95 period. OFFER clearly made large efforts to rectify this in the price controls set from 1995 onwards.[11] However, this proved difficult. After an initial price cap determination for 1995, OFFER at the last moment re-opened the review after information revealed by a takeover bid for a distribution company in late 1994 showed the companies to be more financially powerful than had been apparent at first. This then gave the regulator the information needed to set a more equitable (stringent) price control from 1995 onwards and, at least temporarily, overcame the inherent problem of regulators being at an information disadvantage to the companies being regulated (an example of asymmetric information). The change has been remarkable. For two successive years the distributors have had to reduce charges by an average of 14 percent and 11 percent respectively, and to reduce real prices by a further 3 percent annually for the subsequent three years. As a consequence, distribution company profits are now falling for the first time since privatization.[12]

While the distributors were increasing their profits very rapidly during these early years, the generators and National Grid Company were also highly profitable; the combined profit of the industry was approximately UK£3 billion higher in 1994/95 than in 1990/91.[13] This was politically sustainable only because, by coincidence, the main costs of the industry (fossil fuel purchase) were falling rapidly at the same time.[14] Consequently, consumers were left roughly as well-off in real terms as before (with some decline in industrial prices). Without this compensating change in costs, it is doubtful whether the large increase in industry profits would have been easily managed politically. From the regulatory perspective, it is clear that even in a system with a quite powerful and sophisticated regulatory structure, it has proved very difficult to gain adequate control over the monopoly distribution industry, mainly because of the existence of information asymmetry between regulator and regulated.

The Encouragement of Competition

Competition was to become the central organizing idea of the privatized industry, and the new regulator, OFFER, was charged with encouraging competition wherever possible. However, even in a country as committed to the competition idea as the UK, it has not proved easy to introduce really effective competition.

In the generating sector, OFFER had no powers of price regulation. As long as competition was developing, this was envisaged as an area of very light regulation. In practice, things have been quite different.

First, the initial structure was unpromising. The generating part of the CEGB had been broken up but only into two private companies. This gave them substantial market dominance, and very little genuinely competitive behavior was observable between the two companies in the generating market.[15] As a result, generation has been the subject of virtually continuous regulatory activity. This included a price cap on Pool (wholesale) electricity prices between 1994 and 1996, and the compulsory divestment of 6000MW of capacity by the two large generators. With the market providing limited spontaneous competition, regulatory activity has been substantial but has not yet provided a full solution.

It is often pointed out that a handicap in England was the creation of only two large private generators rather than four or five; while this is a valid argument, it is difficult to apply to other countries. There are few countries outside the OECD that can realistically split their generating sector into five or more companies without doing violence to scale economies in generation.

In addition, there were several other restrictions placed on the operation of competition in generation. Indigenous coal was protected, on a declining basis, until 1998, and nuclear power was also given special financial arrangements to ensure its survival. There was also strong encouragement to new investment in generation (mainly led by distribution companies), and the new Independent Power Plants (IPPs) were allowed to enter into power purchase agreements of 15–18 years with the distribution companies that largely owned them. This put almost all of the new generation outside any competitive market process. One important result of these restrictions was a severe limitation on the role of the Pool as a meaningful price setting device – the real price of generation was being determined elsewhere for virtually all electricity traded.

In the retail supply sector, there is no doubt that competition has been quite successful in the large, mainly industrial market. All users with a maximum demand above 100kW have had free choice of supplier since 1994; after some teething problems, this has worked well. There is now effective competition in this market – covering almost half of all electricity sold – and the need for regulatory intervention is small. In 1998 and 1999, the British market is to be thrown open to full competition, and all 25 million consumers will have a choice of supplier. This provides another example of the need to regulate competitive processes. Issues of security of supply and supplier of last resort, and of equity between consumers, mean that OFFER will need to take a more active role than was necessary when the distribution companies had franchises for household supply. OFFER has also imposed price controls on the domestic market for the first two years of competitive operation.

Implications for Other Countries

Much of this chapter has concentrated on those aspects of the English experiment which have been less effective. This is not an argument that the English experiment has failed. In fact, it has had some very encouraging results in a number of important areas. Two that deserve mention are the genuine independence and transparency of the network, which has encouraged a large volume of highly efficient new gas-based generating investment, and the effective introduction of retail competition for relatively large consumers.

Apart from redressing a situation in which the problems of the new English system are often glossed over, the reason for stressing some of the limitations of the English experience is to show that even where the political will to privatize is strong, and the industry is experiencing no major structural problems, it is not easy to achieve immediately favorable results in all areas of reform. In countries where the industry has larger current problems, or where it faces significant structural problems in the future (e.g., the need for large expansions in capacity), the prospects for imme- diately implementing the appropriate reform are probably less promising. This argues strongly against the "big bang" approach to privatization.

A related lesson is that fundamental reform is a long process, even when it starts with a "big bang." The official timetable for full liberal- ization was always at least eight years – in 1998 coal subsidies end, and all consumers begin to have free retail choices – but in practice it will take even longer to achieve the new structures. Certainly OFFER will continue to watch the household market for several years, regulation of trans- mission and distribution will continue indefinitely, and generation is a continuing subject of regulatory concern and action. This means that privatization needs to be seen as a long process rather than as a discrete event, even where a "big bang" approach is taken.

The third lesson is that there are serious limits to competition in elec- tricity supply. In generation, the size and market power of companies is always likely to be substantial. In the English case, four or five generators could have been created rather than two; however, the capital intensive nature of the industry means that prospective investors need some pro- tection against market risks. Too much competition makes such risks unacceptably high, and the result is that wherever growth in electricity systems is needed, a high degree of competition in generation is difficult to sustain. In retail sales of electricity, competition can be relatively easily introduced for larger consumers, but moving to smaller consumers, the introduction of competition becomes costly and needs close regulation for equity and supply security reasons. Unpicking cross-subsidies is eco- nomically efficient but may lead to unwanted results, especially if richer consumers end up paying less for electricity than their poorer neighbors.

The remaining lessons concern the issue of regulation. A clear impli- cation of almost all that has been argued above is that privatization of electricity must be accompanied by strong and politically independent regulation. The idea of deregulation is simply unrealistic; companies inevitably have a high degree of market power even in potentially com- petitive parts of the industry, and the network remains a monopoly for a very long time. The idea that privatization in electricity is part of "rolling back the state" is therefore impractical, and the corresponding need is to design an effective regulatory system free of some of the traditional kinds of unhelpful political interference that the electricity industry has experienced in many countries, including the UK.

Even when – as in England – the regulator has been given strong powers, is technically competent, and has had tacit political support, it has proved difficult to gain effective control over the industry. Regulators need time to learn, and while they are learning, the economic results are not always as expected. OFFER has learned to be a more effective regulatory force, but it has taken several years and the problem of information asymmetry cannot be fully overcome. The industry as a whole in England made very large profits in the early 1990s, and it is only since 1996 that consumers have – mainly through more effective regulatory intervention – begun to claw back a share of the very large economic gains made available within the industry by the sharp fall in primary fuel prices.

Nor can regulation be seen as merely a transitional process, necessary only until the market is properly organized. The level of competition in electricity is always likely to be quite limited; this requires regulatory scrutiny even in the potentially competitive areas of generation and retail supply. And while technological change may reduce the extent of the natural monopoly elements of the industry – the network of transmission and distribution – this will at best remain a very long-term process. For some decades to come, regulation of the network will remain a vital regulatory function.

All this suggests that privatization needs to be approached with due caution and that it is usually unwise to change too many elements of a system simultaneously. The reform process is lengthy, and in electricity it is not possible to expect the market to take over from the state in all relevant decisions. Regulation is both vital and difficult, even in the relatively favorable circumstances of a country like the UK. Outside the OECD countries, regulation may well prove even more difficult – although without good regulation, it will be difficult to control the economic and political results of privatization.

CHAPTER 7

Privatization: Lessons from the British Experience

Colin Robinson

Introduction

Privatization means different things to different people. Sometimes it is no more than the injection of private capital into projects which are essentially devised and operated by government entities. In other cases, privatization has a more radical meaning: the sale of government-owned assets, either to the public or to existing private companies, so that private property rights are created. The new organizations resulting from this form of privatization may be wholly in private hands or the government may retain a share.

Sometimes there is confusion between privatization and market liberalization. Privatization can proceed without any initial liberalization; the new private organization may have a monopoly, though it will find retaining that monopoly difficult unless there is some government enforced barrier to entering the relevant activity. Liberalization may also proceed without privatization; freeing imports, allowing private firms to enter an industry where there is still a state-owned company, or reducing government regulations which constrain competition ("deregulation") are all examples.

This chapter begins by briefly describing the worldwide trend of privatization. Sometimes these privatizations were accompanied by liberalization; sometimes not. Liberalizing measures per se are less easily described than the progress of privatization, except by listing in detail steps which have been taken in various countries to increase the scope of competitive markets.

The main part of this chapter discusses how and why the privatization movement started, the intellectual basis on which it rests, the errors which have been made as well as the advances in thinking about the subject, and the specific issues which arise in energy privatization. The British experience will be the prime example, as privatization began in Britain. Lessons will be drawn about how countries now contemplating the sale of state assets can achieve the benefits of privatization while avoiding some of the more serious mistakes which were made in Britain.

The Worldwide Spread of Privatization

Britain is generally regarded as the home of privatization, just as 40 years earlier it had been a leading nationalizer. Though other models are emerging as privatization spreads, the OECD noted:

> The United Kingdom by its persistent action over a decade created a framework for the planning and execution of privatization programs in an advanced industrial economy with well-developed capital markets, which would serve as a model for other countries at later times.[1]

After small beginnings in Britain in the early 1980s, privatization blossomed into a worldwide movement. In many parts of the developing world, including central and eastern Europe, as well as in the industrial countries, there are ambitious privatization programs. The International Monetary Fund (IMF) and the World Bank have been influential in spreading privatization; in recent years, they have usually supported it as an integral part of the process of economic reform in developing countries. In central and eastern Europe also, the transition from a state-run to a market economy implies that privatization is an essential component of economic reform programs.

Privatization is no longer a policy of the "right" rather than the "left;" indeed, such short-hand descriptions of political parties have little meaning today. A Labour government in New Zealand was an ardent privatizer. In Britain, though the Labour Party opposed most privatizations carried out by Conservative governments, it shows no inclination to reverse any of them. Indeed, it may even implement others.

One way of measuring the size of privatization programs is by estimates of the revenues raised. The measure is not entirely satisfactory. It implies that the principal aim of privatization is revenue-raising, which is incorrect. Moreover, revenues raised are partly a function of the form of privatization, e.g., whether it is a public-private partnership or the sale of state assets. If state assets are being sold, revenues will depend on whether a government distributes vouchers to citizens or whether it attempts to maximize proceeds from the sale of state assets. Nevertheless, estimates of revenues raised in different countries are useful measures of the extent of privatization, provided one is aware of their deficiencies.

According to recent estimates by the OECD, the amount raised by privatization in 1997 is likely to be almost US$100 billion, compared with US$30 billion in 1990 (see Table 7.1).[2] The main privatizers in the OECD area in recent years have included some of the developing country members of the Organisation as well as the more economically advanced members. Australia, France, Germany, Italy, Japan, Poland, Portugal, Spain, Turkey, and the United Kingdom have all been large-scale privatizers. Mexico had an extensive program in the early 1990s.

Table 7.1
Country Breakdown of Global Amount Raised from Privatization

Country	1990	Estimated 1997
Australia	19	7100
Austria	32	1600
Belgium	—	900
Canada	1504	2000
Czech Republic	—	700
Denmark	644	100
Finland	—	100
France	—	5300
Germany	—	2600
Greece	—	1500
Hungary	38	1000
Italy	—	6600
Japan	—	8700
Korea	—	1700
Mexico	3124	1900
Netherlands	699	600
New Zealand	3895	1839[1]
Norway	—	200
Poland	62	3500
Portugal	1092	3500
Spain	228	11,500
Sweden	—	1100
Turkey	486	4100
United Kingdom	12,906	3300
Total OECD	24,729	69,600
Other Countries	5078	30,000
Global Total	29,807	99,600

Note

1 Figure for 1996.

Source: OECD *Financial Market Trends*, March 1997.

As Table 7.1 indicates, privatization has become increasingly popular outside OECD countries. Some 30 percent of the estimated 1997 total privatization proceeds are expected to be in non-OECD countries, compared with only 17 percent in 1990. Outside the OECD, the biggest privatization programs have been in Brazil and Peru. There has been some privatization in Indonesia, and a program may soon begin in South Africa.

Typically, governments have begun their privatization programs by selling companies which were already operating in competitive markets and which required little restructuring before being offered for sale. Manufacturing companies and financial institutions have therefore often been first on the list. Later, telecommunications – a very popular candidate for privatization in recent years – and other "public" utilities have been sold. These are more complicated cases because some restructuring is generally needed and a regulatory framework usually has to be devised.

Governments have had many motives for privatization. Sometimes countries have been hoping to realize efficiency gains in moving from state to private ownership; wider share ownership has often been an objective; or budgetary strains have induced some governments to privatize in order to ease pressure on the public purse. In other cases, governments have hoped, through privatization, to develop equity markets. Some of the advantages in principle of moving from state to private ownership will be examined, along with the good and bad features of energy privatization British style.

The Origins of Privatization in Britain

In the early 1980s, 40 years after the nationalization program of Clement Attlee's first postwar Labour government, Conservative governments led by Margaret Thatcher began to deregulate and to privatize. Local authority houses were offered for sale to their occupants, and some central and local government services were contracted out to the private sector.[3] But the centerpiece of the Thatcher program was denationalization of the utilities and other "commanding heights" of the economy which Attlee had nationalized. These denationalizations were the most significant change in Britain's industrial policy since the 1940s. They have had reverberations all around the world as other countries have followed suit.

One of the myths about privatization in Britain is that it was a carefully considered and well sequenced program which had been devised by the Conservative Party during its years in opposition. Privatization certainly had been discussed and recommended by Conservative study groups but in practice the "program" began with a series of *ad hoc*, rather tentative steps in which relatively small state-owned companies already operating in competitive markets were sold, in whole or in part, mainly by public flotation.[4] Not until November 1984, with the government well into its second term, did it embark on a major utility privatization, that of British Telecom. Only after that privatization proved very popular with the electorate did the Conservatives move decisively forward with privatization of, *inter alia*, gas, electricity, water, the railways, coal, and nuclear power.

The tentative nature of early privatization efforts is hardly surprising. At the time, the government was feeling its way forward through the fog which surrounds decision-making when the views of the electorate on an issue are unformed.[5] The rationality of voter ignorance (because of the high costs of gathering relevant information compared to likely benefits) tends to make voters ill informed on new, complex issues. The natural response of government is to conduct small-scale experiments with a new policy in an attempt to gauge voter reactions before it decides whether or not the policy should be adopted.

Privatization and its Antecedents

For a major change such as privatization to occur, two principal conditions must be fulfilled. First, there must be some pressing problems which confront a government which it feels can be addressed successfully by the new policy. If this first condition does not hold, no action can be expected. Without the pressure of events, a government, like any other organization, will sense no urge to act, especially since it will feel constrained by its uncertainty about the citizens' views.

In Britain in the 1980s, there were three pressing issues which precipitated action. The first was the perceived need to reduce state borrowing at a time when governments were wary of increasing tax rates because it seemed that the taxable capacity of the electorate was being approached. Second, there was the widespread feeling that the nationalized industries were technologically backward, inefficient, unresponsive to consumers, and forever in conflict with government – in Jack Wiseman's memorable words, they had moved from being the "commanding heights" to the "abysmal depths" of the economy.[6] The final issue was the unpopularity of the public sector trade unions after widespread strikes in a notorious "winter of discontent."

There is, however, a second condition necessary for change. Policy change implies not just government desire and willingness to act but also the presence of an alternative policy capable of being adopted. In other words, the intellectual ground must have been laid for the new policy and some of the practical details must have been worked out.

The intellectual basis for privatization was provided by the counter-revolution in the economics profession in the 1970s, especially in Anglo-Saxon countries. In this case, "counter-revolution" means the move away from the apparent certainties of economic planning (whether of the "command and control" or "indicative" variety), which had so dominated economic policy in the 1950s and 1960s, back to earlier classical liberal ideas. The counter revolution rested both on empirical evidence about the poor – and often perverse – results of state action, and on theoretical ideas about the advantages of using markets and the disadvantages of government intervention.

Economists working in different fields – monetary economics, industrial economics, public choice, or Austrian economics, for example – argued persuasively that government activity had grown under its own momentum rather than because of public demand. It was claimed that government had become too big in many countries, acting as a drag on economic efficiency. A new consensus appeared that governments were pretending to be able to accomplish things they could not do, such as successfully fine-tuning the economy by fiscal means and improving economic performance by selective intervention in industry and commerce; they were suppressing the adjustment capacities of markets; and they were acting more for the benefit of those in government than those governed.[7] Given this new consensus, privatization came naturally to the agenda while state ownership seemed out of place.

The Inherent Problems of State Ownership

Britain's experience of state ownership in the 1940s began with high hopes but such hopes were soon dashed, not so much because of the form nationalization took in Britain but because of the problems inherent when major industries are in state hands.[8] Under state ownership, it is very difficult to provide incentives for managers, the industries concerned tend to be inefficient relative to their private sector counterparts, and consumers are usually not well served.

At the time of nationalization in Britain, Herbert Morrison, its main architect in the Labour government, believed that "public interest" objectives could be identified which the industries would be able to pursue:

- Government would maintain an arm's length relationship, concerning itself only with broad policy issues and leaving the boards it had established to run the corporations on a day-to-day basis;
- Efficiency would improve;
- The rate of technological progress would quicken; and
- Labor relations would be more harmonious than they had been under private ownership.[9]

In practice, none of these desirable developments occurred. Because "public interest" objectives are virtually impossible to identify, the managers of nationalized corporations suffered from serious confusion of objectives. They were unsure whether they were supposed to be operating "commercially" or whether they should have other aims in mind. Governments did not help. They interfered continuously in pursuit of political goals, second guessing managers who felt they were not permitted to manage, and therefore lost their sense of responsibility for the actions of their corporations. Suffering from a lack of appropriate incentives, the industries were inefficient, often technologically backward and unresponsive to consumers. Labor relations were generally very poor, partly because it was believed that, in the end, the government would give way to demands from public sector unions.

Underlying these difficulties were a number of fundamental problems which tend to afflict state-owned industries everywhere. Their principal sources are the absence of well-defined property rights and the lack of competitive markets.

Because the major British nationalized corporations (including gas, electricity, and coal) had state-granted monopolies, consumers lacked the power of exit. Companies like the British nationalized corporations, which knew they had captive customers, behave quite differently from companies whose customers have the power to choose another supplier. The nationalized corporations had little incentive to take consumers' views into account, to cut costs, to keep down prices, or to innovate in the provision of products or services.

The corporations could neither be taken over nor go bankrupt. They were financed by the state and lived outside the market for corporate control, with no quoted share price and no threat from alternative teams of managers to stimulate improvements in internal efficiency. The ultimate "owners" were the voting public but they had no transferable property rights – what was "owned" by everyone was perceived to be owned by no one.

A monopoly in the product markets translated into considerable bargaining power for powerful unions in the nationalized sector, and these unions secured very favorable terms for their members and therefore inflated costs.

Decisions were heavily politicized. Politicians could not resist interfering in industries for which they were thought to have responsibility. Investment programs and prices were influenced – and, at times, controlled – by governments. For example, in the 1970s, Labour governments held down nationalized industry prices in the belief they could thereby reduce the rate of inflation; in the 1980s, the Conservatives made the industries increase prices to reduce public borrowing. The electricity industry was a particularly bad case of extensive interference. Governments dictated which fuels the industry should use for generation – British coal and British-designed nuclear plants were favored – and expected the industry to buy British plant and equipment.[10] Consequently, the industry suffered from severe inefficiencies in its use of inputs, the extent of which was only revealed after it had been privatized.

A succession of White Papers (government discussion documents) on the nationalized industries (in 1961, 1967, and 1978), which dealt with economic and financial targets and relations with government, did little to help.[11] Well-meaning pronouncements, such as those in the 1967 White Paper – the injunction to price on the basis of long run marginal cost and to adopt test rates of discount similar to those used for private sector low risk projects – were over-ridden by the political calculus, a lack of will in the nationalized corporations and by the theoretical and practical difficulties of applying such concepts. The problems were more fundamental than could be overcome by marginal changes to government policy.

Marginal cost pricing in particular is of little use when applied to state monopolies; apart from the almost insuperable difficulty of deciding what costs (and the relevant technology) might be in the long run, there is nothing in economic theory to demonstrate that it is desirable to align prices on the costs of a monopolist.

Advantages of Privatization

In principle, privatization can remedy the problems of state ownership for three main reasons. First, it is a means of lifting the prohibition on entry which frequently accompanies state ownership (though entry restrictions can be lifted to some extent while an industry is state-owned, for example, by freeing imports). Actual and threatened entry to the industry will enhance rivalry, leading to increased efficiency pressures on the companies, faster technological advance and reduced costs which, because of the force of competition, should be passed on to consumers in the form of lower prices and improved standards of service.[12] The need for contrivances, such as marginal cost pricing, is thus eliminated.

Second, the new companies have private shareholders who are much more effective at imposing pressures for enhanced internal efficiency than a Finance Ministry can ever be. Where privatized companies are quoted on stock markets, they will move into the market for corporate control and will be concerned about the possibility of takeover if their share prices decline due to poor performance. They will no longer have the incentive which exists under nationalization to use scarce resources in political lobbying; they will be more inclined to concentrate on lowering costs. Thus, the efficiency gains from privatization can be very large.[13] The most striking example in Britain is the two privatized electricity generators, which have reduced their labor forces by about 70 percent in the seven years since privatization, which is far more than even the greatest optimists about privatization expected.[14] There was no way the British government under nationalization could have known there was such scope for cost cutting. It had no example of a private company operating in a competitive market to guide it in assessing what an efficient generator might look like. Only when markets were operating so that the companies were under pressure from competitors and from shareholders was the model of an efficient generator discovered.

Third, politicization is reduced. In Britain, the nationalized regime was one in which industries were regulated by back door pressures from ministers and civil servants on senior executives. The result was considerable uncertainty about the rules, constant changes of direction by government, and low morale because managers were unable to manage. That old regime has been replaced by a more open system of independent regulatory offices. It has its failings, but it makes the rules of the game clearer and it reduces the opportunities for political interference. Furthermore, the protectionist energy policy which British governments operated for many years – which *inter alia* involved insisting that the state-owned generator favored British-produced coal and British-designed nuclear power stations – also proved unable to withstand privatization of electricity and the other energy industries. The consequences have been much reduced fuel input prices for the privatized generators, removal of an absurd ban on the use of natural gas in power generation, and generally lower energy prices.

In summary, the effect of privatization is to move the companies concerned into competitive capital and product markets. Management of the privatized company should then feel two threats which keep it on its toes, enhancing efficiency and passing efficiency improvements on to consumers in terms of lower prices and better services. The first threat (from the capital market) is the prospect that it might be replaced by an alternative management team if it does not perform well. The second (from the product market) is that competitors might enter its market.

Product market does not mean a "perfect" market which, by definition, cannot exist.[15] The key feature of a competitive product market is simply freedom of entry. Provided the company or companies in a market feel a credible threat of entry, they will bend their efforts not just to holding down costs but to finding ways of retaining existing customers and attracting new ones. Freedom of entry for competitors leads to the power of exit for consumers. Customers with a choice of supplier have the option to move elsewhere if dissatisfied with their existing supplier.

In such a product market, a competitive process will operate which is quite unlike the long run equilibrium of perfect competition (which is a state evidently reached via competition but in which competition has been exhausted). Companies, operating in rivalrous conditions, will behave entrepreneurially, seeking profit opportunities and constantly discovering new ways of satisfying customers. Disequilibrium will be the norm because the status quo is constantly being upset by entrepreneurial activity.[16]

Energy Privatization in Britain: What Could Have Been Done Better?

All of Britain's energy industries are now in private hands apart from a small nuclear company, which has retained the early, out-of-date Magnox reactors now deemed unsaleable to the private sector.[17] Gas was privatized in 1986, electricity (apart from nuclear) in 1990, coal in 1994, and most of nuclear power in 1996. The oil industry in Britain has always been essentially in private hands, though from early this century there was a government shareholding of about 50 percent in British Petroleum (sold in stages in the late 1970s and early 1980s) which never appeared to involve any intervention in management decisions. For a short period in the late 1970s, there was also a state oil company (BNOC, later privatized as Britoil) which operated in competition with private companies.

Energy privatization in Britain has been written about elsewhere, with analyses of what was good and bad about it.[18] To summarize, the biggest failing was the emphasis placed by the government on raising revenue and widening share ownership and the consequent low priority given to introducing competition into the relevant product markets. In gas, and to a lesser extent electricity, the incumbents were transferred into the private sector with a good deal of market power. It has taken many years of action by the industry regulators and the general competition authorities to inject a degree of competition which could have been there from the beginning. The problem was compounded by the government's insistence on retaining "golden shares" in privatized companies, thereby reducing the takeover threat (though, in practice, the Conservative government allowed many takeovers, notably in electricity supply and distribution, to take place).

In the long view, the failure to liberalize product markets in the early days may not appear of great significance. Provided entry to product markets is freed and capital markets are allowed to work without serious obstruction, it can be argued that liberalization will occur naturally; freeing entry is the crucial condition for competitive market processes to work. However, in the case of large industries, which have been state-owned for many years, whose operations affect many people and which are very much in the public eye, the danger of slow liberalization is that political forces will emerge which threaten the liberalization process.[19]

In Britain, the failure to introduce competitive markets from the beginning in gas, electricity, and the privatized industries meant that the initial gains from privatization were concentrated on senior managers and shareholders. Larger consumers, which are powerful pressure groups both in their producer and their consumer roles, also received some early benefits. However, in general, there was insufficient competition to pass on to smaller consumers the efficiency gains from privatization. Therefore, concern grew that the main beneficiaries were "fat cat" managers and shareholders, and there was some backlash against privatization itself.

The consequences of this backlash are as yet unclear. One possibility is that the demands for more prescriptive regulation, which inevitably arise in such circumstances, will be translated into action by the government. The Labour government is reviewing the system of regulation and, since its early actions (the imposition of a "windfall tax" and some decisions about takeover bids) suggest it is more inclined to intervene in that system than was the Conservative Party, it may be that the result will be more regulation and less competition. If regulation is regarded as a last resort which should be reserved only for circumstances in which competitive markets are not feasible, such an outcome is unfortunate.[20]

The main problems which arose from the failure to liberalize markets at the time of privatization are now past. The government should allow competition to develop in electricity, gas, and elsewhere as it is now doing. This is not the time to revert to greater regulation.

But British experience demonstrates the unintended consequences of government action. Privatization schemes which were designed to achieve political objectives (revenue raising and widening share ownership) after a few years unleashed political forces which threaten reregulation and repoliticization of the privatized industries.

Therefore, privatization programs should, always and everywhere, be directed primarily at starting competitive processes in the relevant markets. Where governments give priority to revenue raising, there will be a tendency to leave the privatized companies with substantial market power because, *ceteris paribus*, greater market power will lead to expectations of higher earnings and consequently to enhanced expected revenues from the sale. But, if the objective is to benefit consumers, competition not revenue raising should be the principal aim.

Good Features of Energy Privatization in Britain

Although from the beginning, the form that energy privatization took in Britain has been criticized, the general idea of privatizing the energy industries was correct for the reasons of principle given earlier.[21] Indeed, there was one very important insight in privatization of the British energy and other network utilities which has been of great significance as privatization programs have emerged all around the world. It has also influenced – in a generally beneficial direction – the manner in which regulation of the energy industries takes place.

This insight is the realization that industries at one time regarded as "natural monopolies" – such as gas, electricity, water, telecommunications, and railways – contain large, potentially competitive sectors. The only naturally monopolistic parts (and those only with existing technology) are the networks of wires, pipes, or tracks. Production of gas and electricity, and the supply of these products to consumers can be competitive. Thus, it is perfectly possible – and very desirable, given that competition is the only sure way to safeguard the interests of consumers – to have competition over a common network. Producers compete to put their products into the network, and they (and other suppliers) compete at the other end of the network to supply those products to customers. The network can have a single owner (as do the British gas and main electricity transmission networks) but it may be desirable to have more than one owner. The networks can, for example, be divided regionally so as to provide some yardstick competition and so that extensions can be built by newcomers.

This insight – that substantial parts of "network industries" are potentially competitive – is a genuine innovation. It has made possible something which even ten years ago would not have been thought feasible: the provision of choice of gas and electricity supplier to even the smallest consumers. As already explained, the attitude of suppliers to customers who are no longer captive is likely to change fundamentally and will have beneficial results in terms of lower prices and better service standards.

It follows from the idea of introducing competition where it is feasible that regulators, apart from supervising the transition to competition, should confine their activities purely to the networks. Where competition reigns, regulation is unnecessary – and is indeed likely to be harmful because it will invariably suppress competitive processes. So, as the transition to competition is accomplished, it is desirable that regulation withers away over time. Imbued with these insights, British utility regulation has taken a turn which seems very desirable as compared with regulation in the US. It now presents an alternative model of a regulatory system, with the following characteristics.[22]

Regulatory offices are independent of direct political control. That is a big advance on nationalization, under which managers were constantly being second-guessed by their political masters. The privatized industries are no longer instruments of state policy. A necessary condition for competitive markets to develop was removal of the form of political control which always seems to accompany nationalized ownership.

Instead of attempting to control profits via rate of return regulation, which encourages "gold-plating," prices are controlled under a price cap "RPI minus x" system, which has better incentive properties and is more closely consistent with competitive markets.[23] A price cap regime is to some extent arbitrary (as is all regulation) and it may tend to revert to rate of return regulation if the regulators look primarily at profits in setting 'x' and alter the cap frequently. But, if reviews of the cap are infrequent (say, every five years), it has a very desirable property. Because it allows the regulated companies to retain unanticipated cost savings between reviews, therefore giving them an incentive to improve efficiency, it is the regulatory equivalent of Schumpeterian competition.[24] Instead of Schumpeter's "gale of creative destruction" extinguishing profits, that task is performed by the next regulatory review.[25]

The third innovative feature is the duty to promote competition which, in one form or another, British utility regulators have. Perhaps the government gave regulators this duty not fully aware of its significance. Indeed, there was an accidental element in its imposition in gas.[26] Moreover, the duty has become important partly because the government failed to liberalize markets more at the time of privatization; more liberal schemes would have meant correspondingly less need for liberalizing action by regulators. But the pro-competition duty has become a key feature of the regulatory regime for privatized utilities. Regulators have been able to take action to stimulate entry and to start competitive processes outside natural monopoly sectors even in very unpromising circumstances (such as the early days of privatized gas). The incentives of regulators have also been changed by the presence of this duty so that capture by producers or others is not the issue in Britain that it has been in the US.[27] When one of the principal duties of the regulator is to promote competition, the interests of consumers must be to the fore and the chances of his or her succumbing to the lobbying of producers is much diminished.

Other countries have taken rather different routes in devising regulatory systems for their privatized industries. For example, in New Zealand, which has been remarkably bold and innovative in its economic reforms, an attempt has been made to avoid specific industry regulators.[28] Instead, New Zealand is trying to rely on general competition law. Different routes still are being taken in Australian states such as Victoria, where a number of regulatory innovations are in train. But the point is that the British example stimulated other countries to think further about regulation rather than slavishly following the US example. As a result, there is now some competition among regulatory systems which is very desirable since it helps countries discover which regime best suits their circumstances.

General Comments on Privatization

There are important lessons which can be learned from the British experience by countries which are contemplating privatization, especially of their energy sectors.

First, it is helpful to clarify from the beginning the objectives of privatization, even if it is going to take time to achieve them. This is an area in which Britain failed. The Thatcher government more or less stumbled into privatization of key industries in Britain without any clear view of their aims other than a general desire to reduce the influence of the state.

Privatization is or should be primarily a means of moving state-owned companies into competitive product and capital markets. That is, privatization and liberalization are complementary policies. More specifically, product markets, if not already competitive, should be liberalized, and property rights in the new companies should be clearly defined. They should have private shareholders and be in a market for corporate control.

An almost certain consequence is some de-politicization. It is more difficult for politicians to intervene when there are clear property rights (on which government intervention would encroach) and competitive markets (where intervention may result in increased monopolization and hence higher prices and lower service standards).

Other privatization objectives – such as raising revenues for the government or widening share ownership – are secondary, and indeed are dangerous if given top priority since they are likely to conflict with liberalizing product and capital markets – the objective which should have primacy.

Liberalizing product markets and ensuring that companies exist within a market for corporate control seem to be complementary policies. Not only will they produce strong pressures for internal efficiency, but there will also be incentives to pass efficiency gains on to consumers in lower prices and better standards of service. Without such benefits for consumers, there will be pressures – of the kind now emerging in Britain – to reregulate the industries to avoid "excessive" gains for senior managers and shareholders as they appropriate the efficiency benefits of privatization.

Even if a state-owned company already operates within a product market which is competitive internationally (such as oil), the presence of private shareholders is a necessary discipline to promote internal efficiency and to prevent the build up of bureaucracy. In energy and other utilities, product markets are generally not competitive but they can be made so by liberalizing the potentially competitive sectors.

A second major point is that if utilities are to be privatized, as they should be given the favorable effects of doing so in Britain and elsewhere, some means of network regulation will have to be found. That regulatory system will then assume great significance; it is capable of making or breaking the privatized regime. It is a mistake to opt for a US-type rate of return regulation. It may be an improvement on nationalization but it is a bureaucratic, legalistic regime subject to regulatory capture; any benefits of moving to it from state ownership are likely to be marginal. The new British regulatory regime is better designed to cope with network industries where competition takes place in production and supply. No doubt it can be improved – as, for instance, New Zealand and the Australian state of Victoria are trying to do – but it forms a good basis for supervising utilities while minimizing the problems of capture and the empire-building tendencies of regulators.

Privatization – the most radical change in government policy towards industry and commerce in decades – is, for good reasons, becoming a worldwide phenomenon. It holds out the promise of substantial improvements in internal efficiency in the privatized organizations. It also offers the prospect of substantial benefits for consumers.

Like all such changes in policy, adapting it to local circumstances is crucial to its success. Countries may wish to proceed at varying speeds, starting off with relatively straightforward means of introducing private capital such as public-private partnerships. But, if a privatization policy is to succeed, it is crucial to set and adhere to some long-term aims; the sale of state-owned assets accompanied by market liberalizing measures seem to be the appropriate objectives.

Learning from the errors of others is important. There is now plenty of privatization experience around the world from which lessons can be drawn. Lessons from Britain, the pioneer in this field, show that many mistakes were made in addition to the successes which were achieved. The trick for other countries is to learn from the mistakes while attempting to emulate the success stories.

CHAPTER 8

Privatization and Deregulation of the Energy Sector in the Gulf Co-operation Council Countries: Pros and Cons

Ibrahim I. Elwan, Achilles G. Adamantiades,

and Khalid A. Shadid

Introduction

The privatization and deregulation of the energy sub-sectors of petroleum, gas, and power is in full swing throughout the world. The economic impact on countries that have implemented privatization programs, such as the United Kingdom and New Zealand, has been positive. The experience has also been positive for those emerging economies that have privatized either their entire energy sector or some of its sub-sectors. Production has become more efficient, the quality of services has improved, and mobilization of foreign direct investments has increased while non-government debt has decreased substantially.[1] More importantly, the privatized enterprises have become net contributors to national revenues. This compares favorably with performance prior to privatization, when reliance on governments for direct fiscal support and guarantees of debt was prevalent. Governments' implementation of policy frameworks for privatization has been the single most important factor in attracting direct foreign and domestic investments.

The increased emphasis on privatization and deregulation is attributable to a global trend towards free trade and a commensurate emphasis on comparative advantage. Barriers to free trade are declining as greater reliance is placed on competition and market forces to set prices and determine priorities for resource allocation. This requires the restoration and maintenance of a fiscal and monetary balance which, in turn, requires rationalization of public sector expenditures and increased mobilization of revenues through broader-based taxation.[2] These factors have changed the role of governments in two ways:

- Governments are placing increased emphasis on establishing and implementing policies required to stimulate growth in the export sectors and on creating the environment for greater mobilization of private sector resources and expertise; and
- Governments are limiting their outlays to non-revenue generating sectors, where the determination of prices for cost recovery from consumers is not practical.

This change in the government's role has had a profound impact on the energy sector. The oil sub-sector, usually an important source of government revenue, has moved towards prices that better reflect world standards. Domestic prices of petroleum products have increased, thus reducing and, in most countries, almost eliminating both direct and in-direct subsidies. Gas and coal sub-sectors, whose outputs often do not justify export, have also experienced price increases to remove market distortions, thus bringing prices more in line with the world price of importable substitutes. As a result, the revenues of producing industries have increased, resource use has become more rational, and energy intensive industries are becoming more efficient.[3]

Globally, the power sub-sector has been most affected by this change in government role. Historically, power development depended on public sector support through budgetary allocations or government borrowing in local and international capital markets. Governments underpriced electricity in order to achieve social or developmental objectives.[4] The new approach to government involvement is to realign electricity tariffs with the economic cost of supply. In most countries, subsidies in tariffs are being eliminated. Indeed, subsidies, if any, are being covered through direct government budgetary allocations or through cross-subsidization among consumer categories. Reliance on public sector financing for new investments is increasingly being phased out and replaced by reliance on capital and credit markets.[5]

The ownership structure in the energy sectors throughout the world is also changing dramatically. In the past, energy was deemed a strategic sector whose ownership and control were vested in the hands of governments. This has now led to massive divestitures to the private sector. Oil, gas, coal, and power enterprises that were in the public sector domain for decades are being privatized, and governments' share in their ownership is diminishing. Governments are relinquishing direct control of enterprises in the energy sub-sectors and focusing more on policy and deregulation.

Framework for Deregulation and Privatization

Deregulation refers to the establishment of policies supported by a legal framework which creates a competitive environment for economic activity. Deregulation ultimately moves economies towards world market based prices for all goods and services; in an increasingly global economy, economic success is dictated by competitiveness rather than government fiscal supports and protected markets. Privatization refers to the change from public to private ownership of productive assets.

DEREGULATION

Deregulation aims to foster competition and reliance on market forces for pricing inputs and outputs and for rationing capital. Restrictions on the movement of goods, labor, and capital are removed, and barriers to entry in the various sectors are eliminated, unless these barriers are dictated by technological constraints. Deregulation policies are supported by a legal and institutional framework that safeguards the interests of consumers, producers, and society at large, and establishes standards and processes, e.g., for the resolution of disputes. In essence, deregulation sets sector policies, creates the institutions, and enacts the laws that together consti-tute the "enabling environment" for the private sector to make economic decisions and to capture the rewards, or bear the costs, associated with these decisions. Government's role in enterprise management and operations is minimized, replaced by a role involving the setting of policy frameworks that allow economic agents to maximize their welfare.[6] Deregulation policies can be applied to an entire economy at once, or they can be initially introduced in some key sectors. Then they can be gradually and systematically broadened to encompass the entire economy. The larger the number of sectors deregulated at one time, the smaller the potential for uneconomic decisions.

PRIVATIZATION

Privatization of an enterprise refers to the transfer of the rights of owner-ship, usually through a sale, from the public to the private sector. Arguments in favor of privatization usually cite the potential for improving efficiency, reducing budgetary support, and reducing the risks borne by governments. Privatization is usually achieved in two ways: divesting existing public sector enterprises to the private sector or assigning the development, finance, and operations of new investments to the private sector. Divestiture can be carried out through the sale of major or controlling blocks of shares of an enterprise to strategic private investors, or through the placement of shares in the capital market for sale to the general public. Strategic private investors generally assume control of the enterprises being privatized. On the other hand, when shares are made available to the general public, either existing management is maintained, or a new management is entrusted with the development and operations of the privatized enterprise.

The privatization of an enterprise can take many forms, but is often categorized as either a one-step, two-step or multi-step process.

One-step Privatization
One-step privatization generally refers to the divestiture of ownership of a public enterprise through the sale of all of the equity to the general public, and involves:
- Corporatization of the enterprise, including a new structure for the board of directors;
- Transfer of ownership;
- Restructuring the management and reporting hierarchy, including the separation of activities that will not be relevant to the privatized firm;
- Restructuring the maturity and pricing of debt in order to determine appropriate debt pricing;
- Valuing the company's assets and its net worth, with a view to setting a level for the equity, the number of shares to be sold, and the price of the offer to the market;
- Audit of all the accounts, and certification of bank accounts, accounts receivable, and accounts payable;
- Determination of the manpower to be retained, and compensation packages for redundant employees; and
- Determination of the taxation regime attributable to the enterprise.

Two-step Privatization
Two-step privatization involves the divestiture of the "controlling block" of shares to strategic investors who assume management control of the enterprise, followed by the placement of shares in the capital market. Improvement in efficiency and overall performance as a result of better management are reflected in the appreciation of share prices. The strategic

investors are often a consortium of international and local firms with technical and financial capabilities. The optimal selection of the strategic investors involves a stringent set of criteria for pre-qualification, after which the pre-qualified firms are invited to bid. Prior to bidding, the enterprises to be privatized are usually corporatized (i.e., their organization structure streamlined, their debt restructured to reflect market conditions, and the debt capitalized in conjunction with the valuation of their assets). These activities are usually undertaken by a set of internationally reputable firms. All financial accounts are audited, and liabilities and rights of the enterprise are reviewed and documented. The pre-qualified bidders are provided with all the information and are allowed to visit the facilities to make their own inspection. Normally, bids are submitted and opened publicly and, after bid evaluation, ownership of the enterprise is transferred, to the extent of the controlling block, to the highest responsive bidder.

A major issue in this kind of privatization is the potential for corporate governance disputes between the strategic investor acquiring a substantial yet minority interest and the government maintaining a majority interest. The former will tend towards increased corporate autonomy, while the latter will seek to maintain control over the existing corporate governance structure and the legal status of the newly privatized entity. A trustee organization, normally a recognized financial institution, can hold government shares and work closely with the strategic investor. This helps to address the potential conflict by making basic decisions, such as those relating to the capital structure of the entity or major capital investments, through a process of constructive consultation.

Multi-step Privatization
Under this approach, public sector enterprises are gradually corporatized while the deregulation framework is being put in place and new investments are undertaken by the private sector. The new investments are owned by special purpose companies whose shares are held by the strategic investors during construction and not more than 49 percent of the shares are sold to the general public, both locally and internationally. The new investments are generally implemented under a BOO, or similar scheme where investors and lenders take project specific risks associated with design, finance, insurance, construction, commissioning, and operations.[7] The government's role is to provide guarantees for its performance under the concession agreements and for the performance of its public sector entities and agencies.

Multi-step privatization or divestiture is particularly applicable where public sector enterprises are involved in activities that are considered, in some countries, to be politically sensitive (e.g., electricity, water, or gas). Multi-step privatization is especially suited to public sector enterprises largely dependent on direct budgetary transfers and subsidized prices for capital and inputs. These often require financial restructuring and substantial increases in their output prices to eliminate the subsidies. At times, however, increases in the level of prices charged to consumers can be politically unfeasible. Consequently, "corporatization" may take time to achieve. Public sector enterprises can only be successfully privatized when they face the same market conditions as private sector enterprises for the mobilization of capital and the pricing of their inputs and outputs.

A major issue of concern in implementing any form of privatization is the pricing of the shares or assets to be divested. Setting the offer prices high to maximize government revenues may result in undersubscription. On the other hand, underpricing the shares incurs financial losses and negative political repercussions to the privatization process. Underpricing results in oversubscription which increases share prices because of excess demand, consequently shifting financial gains to the new shareholders. The experience of a number of countries, such as the United Kingdom, Argentina, and New Zealand, has shown that the impact on government revenues of underpricing share offerings during privatization is minimal since the new shareholders' capital gains are taxed. Privatization is found to be more successful when the process is completed on time, albeit with oversubscription, than the reverse.

Development of the Energy Sectors in the GCC Countries

BACKGROUND

Five decades ago, GCC countries were characterized by dependence on oil revenues produced by international firms with concessions for exploration development, production, and marketing. Very few governments, if any, were directly involved in upstream and downstream operations in the petroleum sector. Gas production was, to a large extent, limited to associated gas, as local and export markets for gas were non-existent. Power supply was limited to the principal urban areas, supplied by small private, municipally or government-owned companies, all operated under contract by expatriates. These power systems were largely isolated with minimal interconnection. Access to electricity was limited by the inadequacy of the infrastructure and consumers' ability to pay.

THE PETROLEUM SECTOR

As revenues accrued to the oil companies and to governments through royalties, licenses, and taxation, the sector experienced rapid development. Sector infrastructure was expanded using state of the art technologies, and local manpower received extensive overseas and on-the-job training. Over time, local staff progressed within the ranks of the oil companies, and the transition in management and manpower from expatriate to national staff was achieved fairly smoothly. Oil companies in the GCC are currently being managed and operated by nationals in accordance with the highest international standards. The existence of a technically and managerially capable national cadre, the availability of financing to attract international expertise as required, reliance on market determined prices, stable markets for output, and revenues in the hands of the GCC governments have all contributed to an environment conducive to the corporatization of the petroleum sector. Governments have been able to use their surplus revenues to either establish nationally-owned petroleum companies or acquire controlling stakes in existing foreign-owned companies. Today, national oil companies in the GCC countries are at the cutting edge of their industry, and a few have already ventured outside their area to exploit potential markets for upstream and downstream activities, such as Kuwait Oil Company (KOC), Petroleum Development Oman (PDO), Abu Dhabi National Oil Company (ADNOC) and Qatar Petroleum Company (QPC). These companies are joint venture owners in a number of upstream and, more importantly, downstream operations throughout the world.

THE POWER SECTOR

Governments in the GCC countries took the lead in developing, managing, and operating the power sector, and in financing the sector from national budgets. The present structure and quality of power company services in the GCC clearly would not have been possible without the role that governments have played in the growth of the sector. Several factors contribute to the leading role of governments in the development of the power sub-sector in GCC countries:

- The increasing demand for electricity stimulated by economic growth coupled with the dispersed nature of the population required substantial front-end investments. Financing these investments was not, in most cases, justified on a strictly commercial basis but was accommodated because electricity was viewed as an essential commodity and as a sign of economic development;
- The financial and technical resources of the existing companies which serviced small, isolated systems were inadequate for modern power systems;
- Transmission and distribution networks were required ahead of the development of markets to accommodate the changing population distribution patterns of rapid urban growth;
- The scarcity of water to meet the demands of a rapidly growing population, including a large increase in the number of expatriates, necessitated the development of power generating facilities that also produced desalinated water; and
- Political pressure to keep the prices of electricity and water at levels deemed acceptable by all consumers.

As of 31 December 1997, the GCC countries had approximately 44,000MW of power generation capacity (see Table 8.1). This capacity is either directly owned and operated by governments, or owned by governments and operated under contract by specialized national and international private companies. These companies depend on national budgets or government guaranteed debt for financing expansion. Their internal rate of cash generation and debt service cover ratios are lower than required to allow them to borrow on the strength of their balance sheets. A worst case scenario for the future was outlined by Mackie for economies where hydrocarbons are a main source of revenues. He argues that since hydrocarbons are a finite resource providing the main source of revenues, governments will need to rationalize subsidies or risk financial collapse and recession.[8] The forecast of new additions to the power generating capacities in the GCC countries by the year 2005 shows an increase of about 19,453MW (see Figure 8.1). Assuming an average cost of US$700,000/MW, the total financing required for power generation and water desalination in the GCC countries between December 1997 and 2005 would amount to US$13.6 billion. This financial requirement raises questions about resource mobilization for the sub-sector, revenue sources, and the impact on the overall absorptive capacity of the capital and debt market in the region, as well as the impact on governments' constrained budgets.

Coverage of operating costs and returns to the companies is achieved in most GCC countries by underpricing the cost of fuels for power generation. Governments of the GCC set the domestic prices for petroleum products and gas at levels that would enable their power and water utilities to cover the cost of production, including returns on investment.

Table 8.1
Electricity Market in the Gulf Co-operation Council States

GCC States	Population Mid-1995 (Million)	Per capita GNP 1995 (US$)	Per capita Production 1997 (kWh)	Demand Growth (%)	Installed Capacity 1997 (MW)	Additional Capacity to 2005 (MW)
Bahrain	0.58	7,840	9,493	5	1,350	399
Kuwait	1.70	17,390	19,022	8	7,762	5,106
Oman	2.20	4,820	4,403	9	1,631	2,519
Qatar	0.64	11,600	18,634	10	1,631	3,882
Saudi Arabia	19.00	7,040	4,345	6	23,960	3,276
UAE	2.50	17,400	10,249	10	7,537	4,271
Total					43,871	19,453

Note

The forecasts are based on the following assumptions: average load factor of 55%, annual installed capacity increase of 4%, population growth rate of 1.25%.

Sources: Electricity data are forecasted based on *Electricity in the Middle East*, Financial Times Publishing, 1995; population and per capita GNP from *World Development Report, 1997*.

Figure 8.1
Additional Capacity by Year 2005

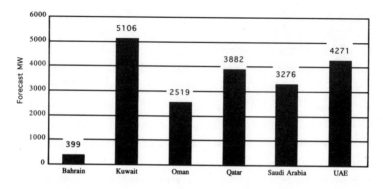

Source: Forecast by Infrastructure Capital Group.

These prices, however, are substantially below the real cost to the economy – the opportunity cost. In the case of petroleum products, the opportunity cost is equal to the border price or the price at which the product could be sold in the international market. As for natural gas, its price is also set below the opportunity cost of the fuels it displaces or its substitutes. The difference between domestic prices and their economic cost constitutes a subsidy to the power sector and, in turn, a subsidy to the consumers of electricity and water. The subsidy is passed on to consumers in the form of electricity tariffs that are below the real cost to the economy.[9] The historical data in Table 8.2 show the 1995 power sub-sector fuel costs in the GCC countries compared to international prices. The difference between the international price and the domestic price of fuel used for power generation is lowest for Oman.

Table 8.2
Production Cost Summary for GCC Member States (1995)

Country	Plant Capacity (MW)	Energy Output (GWh)	Fuel Cost Intl. (US$1000)	Fuel Cost Local (US$1000)	Total Cost Intl. (US$1000)	Total Cost Local (US$1000)	Avg. Prod. Cost Intl. (US$/MWh)	Avg. Prod. Cost Local (US$/MWh)
UAE	5,570	22,639	497,210	208,423	613,295	323,272	23.2	10.4
Oman	1,410	6,609	131,018	124,468	155,138	148,588	21.6	20.6
Qatar	1,860	100,321	112,138	23,586	151,812	51,588	20.3	5.6
Bahrain	970	4,889	100,321	15,129	122,307	37,069	23.4	6.0
SCECO (E)	7,860	39,007	774,843	193,711	866,006	284,834	21.0	6.1
SCECO (W)	5,610	29,058	1,056,353	241,413	1,152,029	333,124	38.9	10.7

Source: Feasibility study, *Evaluation of Electric Energy Trading Benefits within the Mashreq Arab Countries* (vol. 1).

The structures of the petroleum and power sub-sectors in the GCC countries vary because of the role governments and markets have played in their development. This difference determines the speed and the approach to be taken for deregulation and privatization of each sub-sector. In the petroleum sub-sector, deregulation could be achieved in a relatively short time as joint ventures between the private sector and cor-poratized public sector entities are already in place, both upstream and downstream. By contrast, privatization of the power sub-sector is likely to take longer as it would require the deregulation of the sub-sector, the realignment of prices with the economic cost of supply, the allocation of costs between power and water, and the institution of policies for cost recovery through tariffs.

Another fundamental difference between the petroleum and power sub-sectors is in their sources of financing. The petroleum sub-sector is able to mobilize both debt and equity financing in the international capital markets because of its potential for revenue generation through the export of oil or petroleum products at world prices. Revenue generation in the power sub-sector, on the other hand, is based on domestic policies for pricing electricity and water. The adequacy of these tariffs to generate revenues that would cover debt service, operations, and maintenance costs, adequate levels of self-financing for new investments, and competitive returns to investors are the key areas that need to be addressed as a prerequisite to privatization. Since investments in the power sub-sector are lumpy, involving substantial front-end capital outlays and debt financing of long maturities, adequate revenue generation through tariffs, based on sound commercial basis, is essential for sub-sector access to international debt and equity markets.

A Potential Privatization Strategy for the Energy Sector

THE PROCESS OF PRIVATIZATION

Lance Marston, in his paper "Preparing for Privatization: A Decision Maker's Check-List," provides a table summarizing the decision-making process pertaining to the question of whether or not to privatize a public sector enterprise. This decision-making diagram is reproduced in Figure 8.2.

Figure 8.2
Privatization Decision Tree

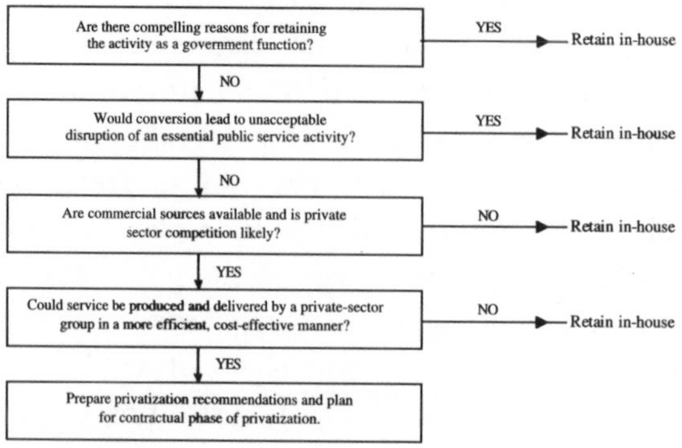

Source: Lance Marston, *Preparing for Privatization: A Decision Makers Check-list.*

Applying this decision tree to the energy sub-sectors of the GCC countries leads to the conclusion that all public enterprises are candidates for privatization. However, since the oil and petroleum enterprises are the principal sources of revenue, their privatization touches on issues of sustainability of governments' resource mobilization. As a result, the strategy for their privatization will differ substantially from that for the other energy sub-sectors.

In the petroleum sub-sector, the structure of the public enterprises is based on vertical integration where enterprises control or have a major stake in exploration and development, refining, and marketing. At the exploration and development level, given the contribution of oil revenues to the national budgets and the fact that most of the exploration and development are undertaken through joint venture arrangements with international oil companies, there is little economic justification for privatization. One could only argue for a financial structure for the oil companies – already in place in most of the countries – that sets market-determined financial performance targets. This provides the means to monitor the financial performance of enterprises which would foster efficiency on the part of their management and promote accountability.

As far as petroleum refining, marketing, and distribution are concerned, these downstream activities could be corporatized. In view of their well established track record, governments could consider selling between 30 and 40 percent of their total equity to the general public as a means of recovering some of the economic rent. This approach is consistent with the two-step privatization scheme, where the first step of having a strategic investor in place has already been achieved.

The critical requirement for the successful privatization of these enterprises is the separation of their debt mobilization from their balance sheets. Each of these enterprises should be restructured to provide them with independent operations, balance sheets, adequately structured debt to equity ratio, cover ratios, and internal contributions toward future investments. Success in the management of the downstream petroleum companies would be determined by the performance of their shares in the local and international markets. This has the advantage of allowing the capital market to evaluate objectively the viability of the companies' management and of providing clear signals to policy makers about the need for change. Changes in management of the corporatized downstream enterprises would be undertaken by their independent boards without interference by governments.

Gas producing public sector enterprises in the GCC countries should be restructured using the same approach proposed for the oil and petroleum enterprises. Where gas is providing the major source of revenue for governments, the public sector enterprises could be retained in the hands of governments, provided there is a corporatization of the enterprises and well-defined indicators of financial performance. These financial performance criteria should be based on prices agreed with governments for retention by the enterprises and the rest of the revenue refunded to the governments. Gas liquefaction and transportation need not be maintained in the public domain. Instead, a two-step privatization approach to structuring these enterprises could be considered, in a manner similar to that outlined earlier for the privatization of oil and petroleum product enterprises.

The privatization of the public sector enterprises in the power sub-sectors in the GCC countries is justified but would require time to be implemented optimally. Substantial work is required in setting up the enabling environment and enacting the policies for the deregulation of the sub-sector. Commercial codes and a legal framework would need to be put in place and new laws drafted and implemented covering such diverse aspects as property rights, personal and corporate taxation, access to capital markets, capitalization, and auditing. In addition, the financing of these enterprises would need to be considered with a view to restructuring them in line with internationally accepted standards. Subsidies in the form of fuel under-pricing should be phased out; cross-subsidization between consumer classes should be eliminated; short-term debt should be refinanced; and new loans with competitive interest rates and maturities should be put in place. Realignment of the debt to equity ratios and the cover ratios would need to be undertaken with a view to strengthening the enterprises' balance sheets, and hence their ability to successfully tap the local and international capital market for both debt and equity.

BOO Schemes for Developing New Power and Water Supply Facilities

In parallel with the sectoral and corporate structure changes proposed for the public sector enterprises, the creation of the institutional framework necessary for developing future investment under BOO arrangements could be considered. The BOO approach to financing investments would require market-based tariffs that would generate revenues sufficient to cover debt service, insurance, operations, and maintenance costs, and to ensure internationally competitive rates of return on investment necessary to attract equity investments in independent power projects (IPPs). IPPs would be required to fund their equity and debt by tapping the capital and credit markets, internationally and locally, without any guarantees of the debt from governments. However, guarantees of the obligations and the undertakings of the public sector enterprises involved in purchasing the output should be provided, as will be discussed below. Private sector involvement in the power sub-sector has contributed to the overall performance of the sub-sector through improved implementation and operational efficiencies. Properly structured IPPs can also stimulate the development of local capital markets and bring the discipline of capital markets to support competition in electricity production.[10]

To enable IPPs to enter successfully in the power sub-sector, an unambiguous private power policy needs to be articulated. A comprehensive institutional enabling environment should be put in place and should include the following elements:

- A legal framework that (a) allows contracts to be enforceable (including mechanisms for the resolution of disputes); (b) provides for the private sector ownership of power assets; (c) empowers a state-owned utility to enter into power purchase agreements (PPAs) with IPPs; and (d) offers assurances of ownership rights to the streams of revenues;
- A tariff structure that would foster efficiency in development and operations, and tariff levels sufficient to cover all costs and debt service and provide a competitive return on investments;
- Policies that encourage local and foreign private investment;
- Clearly defined and delineated roles and responsibilities for inter-ministerial coordination with respect to permits, clearances, and approvals;
- Well-articulated tax laws, import duties, and incentives applicable to both local, state-owned power utilities and IPPs;
- Unhindered access to capital in the form of debt and equity; and
- Well-defined laws for monitoring and mitigating any adverse environmental impact of projects during construction and operations.

A factor to be considered in the privatization of the power sub-sector in the GCC countries is that power utilities are also entrusted with the production of desalinated water, which is not generally the case elsewhere. Corporatization in this case would have to address the issues related to the joint cost of production and the allocation of this cost between power and water consumers. The problem is further complicated by the need for a water pricing structure that provides affordable clean water to all segments of the population, while covering the economic cost of supply.

Allocation of Risks Between Public and Private Sectors

Investments by private sector power enterprises should be undertaken under Limited Recourse Financing (LRF).[11] This would avoid the need for governments to raise the financing for new investments using their balance sheets. Instead, under LRF, lenders and investors rely on the forecast revenues of the enterprises for security that debt service, organization and method costs, company costs, and return on investment will be covered. In order to support the lender reliance on the revenues of new investments, a set of inter-related agreements and provisions aimed at safeguarding the interests of lenders, investors, and governments, referred to as the security package, is put in place for each new investment. Governments are only required to guarantee that their own performance and that of their institutions comply with their undertakings under the security package.

The security package is composed of a set of inter-related agreements and provisions in the form of contracts and service agreements, escrow accounts, letters of credit, standbys, and investor guarantees, all of which are aimed at assuring the government that the project will be designed, constructed, and operated in accordance with accepted international standards. In addition, the security package provides the lenders with the required comfort through recourse and rights to "cure" in the event of default by IPPs. Finally, it safeguards the interests of investors, giving them the right to declare dividends, dispose of equity, and repatriate capital.

Successful IPPs require a balanced allocation of risks between the parties involved in the project: investors, lenders, and governments and their utilities. Risks associated with projects implemented under limited recourse are divided into two categories: sovereign risk and commercial risks.

- Sovereign or political risks: governments usually assume the political and sovereign risks, such as covering the timely payments for output or services, access to the capital market, unrestricted transfer of funds to service debt, remittance of insurance premiums, repatriation of dividend, and unrestricted convertibility of domestic to foreign currency.

- Commercial risks: the private sector assumes the commercial risks covering the design, finance, construction, and operation of the power facilities.

Figure 8.3 illustrates a typical structure for the main agreements comprising the security package for an investment in power generation. The figure also shows the classification of the various agreements under sovereign and commercial risks.

Figure 8.3
Allocation of Commercial and Sovereign Risks

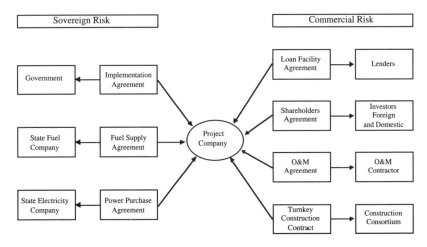

GOVERNMENT GUARANTEES

In infrastructure projects developed by the private sector on an LRF basis, investors and lenders typically look to governments as the ultimate guarantor of the obligations laid out in the agreements to which the government or one of its agencies is a party. The nature of the guarantee is negotiated with lenders where sovereign risks are identified and measures to mitigate them agreed upon. In the case of IPPs, governments often guarantee the payments due to the IPP by the state utility under the power purchase agreement. It also guarantees the availability of foreign exchange for servicing the debt and repatriation of dividends to investors; the quantity, quality, and price of fuel as stipulated under the fuel supply agreement; and the award of consents required for the development of the project, as stipulated under the implementation agreement.

Summary and Conclusions

- The structure of the energy sub-sectors, as they stand today, emerged as a result of the historical market conditions.
- There is potential for deregulation and privatization of the energy sub-sectors (e.g., petroleum, power/water, and gas) which would provide net gains to the economies of the GCC countries.
- The energy sub-sector in the GCC countries is ready for privatization.
- The privatization of the public sector petroleum enterprises downstream can be achieved in a relatively short period of time, as the local capabilities are well developed and operations under conditions dictated by the international markets are well established.
- The privatization of the public sector power/water utilities in the GCC countries will require a relatively longer time than that for the petroleum sector because of the extent of deregulation and reform required to realign the tariffs and cost of inputs to those prevailing in the world markets.
- The development of the concept of BOO for financing new investment could provide the bridging from public ownership to privatization by fostering the institution of laws and policies that will provide the confidence to investors and lenders to undertake, as a start, project related risks in the GCC countries.
- The risks associated with investments in the GCC are sovereign and political risks and commercial risks. Financing new investments under limited recourse would require governments to extend guarantees of their performance under the agreements comprising the security package.

Contributors

ACHILLES ADAMANTIADES is the Director of Engineering at the Infrastructure Capital Group (ICG) in Washington, DC. He has accumulated over 30 years of experience in the power industry, with a specialization in advanced technologies, nuclear safety, research and development, and project evaluation and analysis. Dr. Adamantiades has worked for ten years with the Electric Power Research Institute (EPRI), the premier R&D arm of the US power utilities. He has experience in the operation of thermal power plants with the Public Power Corporation of Greece and extensive academic and research accomplishments, including over 30 technical papers and two books on energy technology. He holds a Diploma in Mechanical and Electrical Engineering from the National Metsovion Polytechnion of Athens, Greece and a PhD in Nuclear Engineering from the Massachusetts Institute of Technology (MIT).

IBRAHIM I. ELWAN is the Chief Executive Officer of ICG. Prior to founding ICG, Mr. Elwan had 18 years of experience at the World Bank in Washington, DC, where he managed the formulation and implementation of policies for the development, deregulation, and privatization of the energy sector, as well as the financing of energy and transport projects in Europe, North Africa, the Middle East, South Asia, and Latin America. He launched the World Bank's Private Sector Energy Development Fund for Pakistan and was the architect of the financial structure for the Hub River Power Project (1,292MW), one of the largest Independent Power Producer (IPP) projects in the emerging markets. Mr. Elwan has a BS in Industrial Engineering and Management from Oklahoma State University and an MA in Economics from the University of Oklahoma.

SHARIF GHALIB is Director of the Sovereign Ratings Group at Standard and Poor's in London. Previously, he was Senior Vice President and Chief Economist of the Gulf Investment Corporation headquartered in Kuwait. Dr. Ghalib holds a BA and MA in Economics from the American University in Beirut and a PhD from Pennsylvania State

University. He has also been a consultant to the Middle East Economic Service of Wharton's Econometric Forecasting Associates, an Assistant Professor of Economics at Pennsylvania State University, and a Research Associate with the United Nations Economic and Social Office in Beirut. He has authored numerous papers and articles in such publications as *Middle East Economic Survey, International Finance, Euromoney, OPEC Bulletin*, and the *Proceedings of the American Statistical Association*.

RAJNISH GOSWAMI is a Senior Consultant for Asia Pacific Energy at Wood Mackenzie Consultants. Between 1994 and 1997, he was a Research Associate for the Tata Energy Research Institute (TERI) in New Delhi, where he was responsible for analyzing the Indian downstream oil and gas industry, petroleum product demand-supply, the competitiveness of the Indian refining industry, LNG in power generation, the economics and potential for gas to power, and India's energy dilemma. He received a Masters in Business Economics from the University of Delhi.

PAUL HORSNELL is the Assistant Director for Research at the Oxford Institute for Energy Studies, and Praelector in Economics at Lincoln College, Oxford. He holds a degree in Philosophy, Politics, and Economics, and a PhD in Economics, both from Keble College, Oxford. His publications include *Oil Markets and Prices: The Brent Market and the Formation of World Oil Prices* (London: Oxford University Press, 1993), co-authored with Robert Mabro; and *Oil in Asia: Market, Trading, Refining and Deregulation* (London: Oxford University Press, 1997).

MICHAEL KUCZYNSKI is an international economist with interests in finance. A graduate of Cambridge University, he was on the research staff of the International Monetary Fund for a decade before returning to Cambridge to direct studies in Economics at Pembroke College. He has numerous publications in the area of foreign investment, international business cycles, and international finance.

GORDON MACKERRON is a leader of the Energy Programme, Science Policy Research Unit (SPRU), University of Sussex. An economist by training, he has been a member of SPRU for 19 years. His research specialty is the economic and policy issues in the international electricity system, including nuclear power. Besides a wide range of academic publications, Dr. MacKerron makes frequent radio and TV broadcasts and has advised many public sector organizations in the UK and internationally, including as a specialist advisor to the UK House of Commons Trade and Industry Select Committee, consultant to the UK electricity regulator (OFFER), and the European Parliament and European Commission. He is currently Chairman of the Energy Panel of the British Government's Technology Foresight Programme.

COLIN ROBINSON is Editorial Director of the Institute of Economic Affairs and Professor of Economics at the University of Surrey. He worked as a business economist for 11 years, first with Procter and Gamble and then Esso Petroleum Company (Head of the Economics Division in the Corporate Planning Department) and Esso Europe (Economic Adviser in the Natural Gas Division). Professor Robinson is a Fellow of the Royal Statistical Society, Fellow of the Institute of Petroleum, Trustee of the Wincott Foundation, member of the Scientific Committee of Energia, and member of the Monopolies and Mergers Commission (Electricity Panel). In 1992, he was named Energy Economist of the Year by the British Institute of Energy Economics. He is the sole or co-author of 23 books and monographs and approximately 150 papers, including studies of North Sea oil and gas, the British coal industry, energy policy and electricity, and coal privatization programs.

KHALID SHADID is a Financial Economist with the Infrastructure Capital Group (ICG), a private project development company, and is involved in developing financial structures and debt financing of ICG's projects. Mr. Shadid received a BA in Business Administration from the American International University in London (Richmond College). He completed a MSc in Economics of Urbanization and Managing the City Economy at the University College, London where he also received a Diploma in Urban Management and Planning Practice.

ABDUL HAFEEZ SHAIKH has over 15 years of experience in privatization and private sector development work. He has led teams of World Bank staff and experts and acted as advisor to Pakistan, Saudi Arabia, Sri Lanka, Thailand, Jordan, Philippines, Ghana, Tanzania, Bangladesh, Vietnam, Argentina, Indonesia, Malaysia, Romania, and other countries. He has been responsible for the design and implementation of national privatization programs and successful completion of transactions in energy, telecommunications, finance, and manufacturing. Currently he is the World Bank Resident Representative in Saudi Arabia and also acts as advisor to the Saudi Government on privatization and private sector development. Prior to joining the World Bank, Dr. Shaikh worked at Harvard University.

LEENA SRIVASTAVA has a PhD from the Indian Institute of Science, Bangalore in the area of Energy Economics. She is currently working as Dean, Policy Analysis Division at the Tata Energy Research Institute in New Delhi. Dr. Srivastava has been with TERI for the last 15 years and was also seconded to their affiliate institute – Tata Energy and Resources Institute – in North America between 1992 and 1994. Dr. Srivastava has several books and research publications to her credit and most recently has been working on a project for the Ministry of Petroleum and Natural Gas in India that is assisting in defining the structure and responsibilities of a proposed regulatory body for the downstream oil sector in India.

ANDREW WARD is a partner in the international law firm Simmons & Simmons. He joined the Simmons & Simmons headquarters in London in 1984 and became a partner in 1992, having specialized in corporate finance and company law. In 1994, he was appointed by the regulator of the UK's privatized gas industry, the Director General of Gas Supply, to advise on the new legislation and regulatory regime required to introduce competition in the supply of gas to domestic consumers in Great Britain. Mr. Ward has a law degree from Churchill College, Oxford.

Notes on the Text

Notes on Introduction

1. As recently as in its 1988 *World Development Report*, the World Bank placed state enterprises at the top of the list of feasible responses to infrastructural problems.
2. Consider for example the various Brady Plan restructurings, together with the associated debt equity swaps, and the general securitization of external exposures in the 1990s.
3. This possibility arises not so much because of appropriate regulation of investments, as because of the competition which – contrary to earlier conventional wisdom – can quite successfully be introduced into sheltered sectors as they are privatized.
4. Although it is incorrect to count an asset sale as if it were income inflow, the contribution of privatization to current budgetary financing is sometimes viewed as a separate point at issue.
5. This belongs to the set of observations in corporate finance formalized by Modigliani and Miller (1958, 1961). It is akin also to what is known as "Ricardian equivalence" in public finance.
6. An economic rent refers to advantages which accrue to ownership of a resource because its value exceeds its cost of mobilization. Under perfect information without transaction costs, the present value to the state of all future economic rents expected from public mobilization of resources can be identified and equalized to the present value of the post-tax proceeds to the state expected from private mobilization.
7. UK experience in this regard is instructive. With a few exceptions, state industrial holdings carried over from World War II into peacetime without inquiry as to what appropriate management objectives might be. Only in 1961 did parliament begin to interest itself in effects on economic performance and the general public. By 1967 this interest crystallized into guidelines which, by emphasizing "allocative efficiency" in pricing and in reckoning the opportunity cost of capital, were implicitly tolerant of loss making and hence of

administrative slack. The drain on the budget which followed ushered in, in 1976, a commercial regime which in effect set the stage for privatization – in which the United Kingdom was thus to lead the world. See also Chapter 7.

8. Although in practice this is generally true, it is nonetheless possible for assets to be privatized at a "fair" or efficient price without windfall to investors, for example if the assets have diversification properties which particular investors are willing to pay for. This is clearly possible in the energy sector.

9. Privatization may leave existing capacity "stranded" in the sense that a plant which would have been productive under one regulatory or non-competitive environment becomes obsolete under deregulation or competition.

10. Effects are of course sensitive to the form of taxation (e.g., sales versus profits tax, with or without depletion allowances) and to its expected change over time.

11. It should be noted that if ancillary foreign private capital participation is thus preferred to basic ownership of deposits, the net effect on national net worth is not necessarily positive. In the case of basic ownership, the investor may bear more of the risk arising from real resource price fluctuation, which in the ancillary/auxiliary case the investor can pass back to the host state.

12. Cost of capital combines debt interest, or bond yield, and return on equity, both evaluated post-tax.

13. Indebtedness, by increasing the probability of insolvency (whereby the management team would lose), may credibly promise a tightening up of managerial performance.

14. Regulation poses both institutional and instrumental problems. Institutionally the United States' formula is that of collegial regulation, with some balance among imperfectly informed consumer, taxpayer, environmental, and other interests (as well as the industry itself) represented within the regulatory body, and allowing it at times to be "captured" by the industry. The United Kingdom, inheriting its approach from a past of state enterprises overseen by a minister responsible to Parliament, has adopted the formula of the individual regulator as arbiter among interests, often unstably sensitive to their sectional pressures. Thus each formula has disadvantages. Instrumentally, the US model has long been regulation of rates of return, which has a well-known bias towards over-capitalization of the

industry (the so-called Averch-Johnson effect). It is not entirely clear that the UK model of regulation of price (to move with retail prices minus an imposed productivity increment) does not share some of the same defects in terms of biasing investment decisions, especially if the period between price reviews is short. In general, of course, regulators cannot be expected to be sufficiently well-informed about the industry whose investment decisions they inevitably affect.

15. A typical problem is that utilities are large in capitalization in relation to the rest of the local capital market, so that they may not be valued correctly (and hence not be disciplined appropriately) by the local market unless – through "globalization" – the local market is really coextensive with the international market.

16. Although the transmission relationship is often treated as akin to point-to-point freight transportation, it is in fact closer to being a reservoir to which the supplier adds and from which the consumer draws off. Transmission losses are common network losses, resembling evaporation.

17. In certain settings, the problem of capacity-diversification in electricity generation has been greatly simplified by combined-cycle gas-fueled plants, capable of efficiency at relatively small size (e.g., 50MW).

18. If there is a possibility that, under fickle regulation or otherwise, customers might repeatedly switch away from ongoing capacities (e.g., from oil-fueled to gas-fueled generators), leaving producers with unremunerated costs, the cumulative result over time may well be not cheaper but more expensive electricity. To avoid such an outcome, the system of regulation and competition needs to build into itself a way of dealing with stranded costs. The capacities which solved yesterday's problems of load should be rewarded for doing so, otherwise investments that would solve tomorrow's problems will be unforthcoming.

19. That said, however, it should be noted that in OECD countries, whether in Europe or North America, such cooperation is still rare, and where utilities are in private hands, national markets can still be seriously segmented through regulatory negligence. As recently as 1996, the Ford Motor Company reported paying for delivery of electricity to its different US plants at prices ranging from US$33 to US$75 per MW/hr for supply on the same non-interruptible basis.

Notes on Chapter 1

1. These estimates, prepared by the Gulf Investment Corporation of Kuwait, are meant to provide the analyst and potential investor with a conservative but realistic projection of likely projects during the next three to five years, not merely a "wish list" of projects.

Notes on Chapter 2

1. The views expressed are those of the author alone and should not be attributed to the World Bank or any of its affiliated organizations.

2. The rate of borrowing 10–15 year money by the Omani government may be 8 or 9 percent, based on reception of Omani five year bonds by the capital markets. However, the private cost of financing for a similar duration for the power sector could be 16 percent or higher in nominal terms. Improvements in the policy regime and credible implementation may reduce this rate by a couple of percentage points, but the figure would still remain higher than rates on sovereign borrowing. However, (a) excessive reliance on public finances may make the fiscal position untenable and the government's limited borrowing capacity has to be preserved for areas where private capital is not readily available; (b) the sovereign guarantees that make the public borrowing cheaper can also be extended to the private sector with similar effects (this option appears to have been rejected by the Omani decree); and (c) the inherent risks of a project are not affected by the choice of financing.

3. Al-Bader, "Kuwait Investment Authority's Experience in Implementing the Privatization Program," paper presented to the seminar on "Privatizations: Previews and Prospects," Kuwait, 1996.

4. Sixty-five percent of QATARGAS is held by the state-owned Qatar General Petroleum Corporation. Other shareholders include Mobil-USA (10 percent), Total France (10 percent), Mitsui Japan (7.5 percent), and Marubeni Japan (7.5 percent).

5. In mixed economies, the share of public enterprises in the GDP ranges between 10 and 15 percent (see Abdul Hafeez Shaikh, *The Rise, Decline and Future of Public Enterprises* [Boston, MA: Harvard University, 1991]).

6. In the case of primary production of oil and gas, a case can be made for public ownership (or at least public involvement) as the optimal

rate of depletion of a natural resource from a national economic point of view may be different from one based on purely commercial considerations.

7. For case studies from UK, Mexico, Malaysia, and Chile, see Galal et al (1993). For cases on Argentina including those in petroleum, gas, and electricity, see Abdul Hafeez Shaikh, *Argentina Privatization Program: A Review of Five Cases* (Washington, DC: World Bank, 1995).

8. For discussion on issues of industry structure see Pierre Guislain, *The Privatization Challenge* (Washington, DC: World Bank, 1997); for Argentinean experience, see Shaikh (1995) op. cit.

Notes on Chapter 3

1. Emiri Decree No. 7 of 1997.
2. Article 2, Constitution of the United Arab Emirates.
3. Article 3, Constitution of the United Arab Emirates.
4. Article 121, Constitution of the United Arab Emirates.
5. Federal Law No. 8 of 1984 (as amended); Federal Law No. 18 of 1993; Federal Law No. 5 of 1985.
6. Article 120, Constitution of the United Arab Emirates.
7. Article 17, Federal Law No. 1 of 1972.
8. Article 148, Constitution of the United Arab Emirates.
9. *Middle East Economic Digest* interview with His Highness Sheikh Dhiyab bin Zayed Al Nahyan, reported 22 August 1997.
10. Article 22, Federal Law No. 8 of 1984.
11. Articles 70–94, Federal Law No. 8 of 1984.
12. Article 7, Federal Law No. 8 of 1984.
13. Articles 152, 153, and 227, Federal Law No. 8 of 1984.
14. Article 12, Federal Law No. 8 of 1984.
15. Articles 164–177, Federal Law No. 18 of 1993.
16. Articles 49–56, Federal Law No. 18 of 1993.
17. Articles 21 and 235, Federal Law No. 11 of 1992.
18. Articles 152, 153, and 227, Federal Law No. 8 of 1984.

Notes on Chapter 4

1. World Development Report, *The State in a Changing World*, (Washington, DC: World Bank, 1997).
2. S.S. Ahluwalia, "Financing energy investment in India – 1998 to 2012: The role of economic reform in bridging the demand-supply gap," proceedings of the 20th International Conference of the International Association for Energy Economics, Volume III, 1997.

Notes on Chapter 5

1. Robert E. Lucas Jr., "Economic Policy Evaluation: A Critique," Carnegie Rochester Conference Series on Public Policy, no. 1, 1976. Also see his *Studies in Business-Cycle Theory* (Cambridge, MA: MIT Press, 1981).
2. The literature on the evaluation of the policies is a large one. However, the best description remains John Vickers and George Yarrow, *Privatization: An Economic Analysis* (Cambridge, MA: MIT Press, 1988).
3. That is not to say that BP was able to operate in complete commercial freedom. The government share did cause constraints, and the government was not always mute on company policy or the composition of its board. See J.H. Bamberg, *The History of the British Petroleum Company vol. 2: The Anglo-Iranian Years 1928–1954* (Cambridge: Cambridge University Press, 1994).
4. "We knew that by our contract we should confer upon the Anglo-Persian an immense advantage which, added to their concession, would enormously strengthen the company and increase the value of their property. If this consequence arose from the action of the State, why should not the State share in the advantage which we created?" Winston Churchill quoted in Henry Longhurst, *Adventure in Oil: The Story of British Petroleum* (London: Sidgwick and Jackson, 1959).
5. Robert Mabro, Robert Bacon, Margaret Chadwick, Mark Halliwell, and David Long, *The Market for North Sea Crude Oil* (Oxford: Oxford University Press, 1986).
6. A case could also be made that in the key energy sector privatizations (most notably gas and electricity), the structure of the privatized

industry was heavily influenced by the twin expediencies of a desire to privatize quickly in the face of opposition and obstruction from the existing management.

7. Jean-Jacques Laffont and Jean Tirole, *A Theory of Incentives in Procurement and Regulation* (Cambridge, MA: MIT Press, 1993).

8. For an excellent treatment of relationships between PDVSA and the Venezuelan government, see Juan Carlos Boue, *Venezuela: The Political Economy of Oil* (Oxford: Oxford University Press, 1993).

9. This taxonomy of regulation was developed and expanded in Paul Horsnell, *Oil in Asia: Markets, Trading, Refining and Deregulation* (Oxford: Oxford University Press for the Oxford Institute for Energy Studies, 1997).

10. Horsnell, op. cit.

11. Ibid.

Notes on Chapter 6

1. The stress on "England" (and Wales) derives from the fact that privatization took quite different forms in England and Wales, in Scotland, and in Northern Ireland. The latter two privatization processes were markedly less radical than that in England and Wales, so that the "UK" or "British" model for electricity supply is normally the "England and Wales" model.

2. Much of the material used in the description of the England and Wales privatization in this paper is taken from J. Surrey (ed.) *The British Electricity Experiment* (London: Earthscan, 1996).

3. A useful discussion of some of the terminology discussed below in a context of developing countries is contained in W. Teplitz-Sembitzky, *Regulation or Deregulation – What is Needed in the LDCs Power Sector* (Washington, DC: World Bank, 1990).

4. A natural monopoly occurs when costs fall continuously as output rises, and so the most efficient solution is to have only one firm producing the relevant output. The transportation functions of transmission and distribution in the ESI are classically natural monopolies. For further discussion of the relationship between the privatization process and natural monopolies, see J. Vickers and G. Yarrow, *Privatization and the Natural Monopolies* (London: Public Policy Centre, 1985).

5. See S. Thomas, "The Privatization of the Electricity Supply Industry" in Surrey (1996) op. cit.
6. From the regulator himself; see OFFER, 1991.
7. Thomas, op. cit.
8. J. Chesshire, "UK Electricity Supply under public ownership" in Surrey (1996) op. cit.
9. M. Beesley and S. Littlechild, "Privatization: principles, problems and priorities," in M. Bishop et al. (eds) *Privatisation and Economic Performance* (Oxford: Oxford University Press, 1994).
10. G. MacKerron and I. Boira-Segarra, "Regulation," in Surrey (1996) op. cit.
11. OFFER, 1996.
12. OFFER, 1997.
13. OFFER, 1993 and 1997.
14. M. Parker "Effects on demands for fossil fuels" in Surrey (1996) op. cit.
15. D. Newbery, "The restructuring of UK energy industries," in G. MacKerron and P. Pearson (eds) *The UK Energy Experience: A Model or Warning?* (London: Imperial College Press, 1996).

Notes on Chapter 7

1. OECD, "Privatisation: Recent Trends" in *Financial Market Trends*, 66 (March 1997).
2. Ibid.
3. A.T. Peacock, "Privatisation in Perspective," *Three Banks Review* vol. 144 (December 1984).
4. Colin Robinson, "Privatising the Energy Industries: The Lessons to be Learned," *Metreoeconomica* vol. 43, no. 1–2 (February–June 1992).
5. Anthony Downs, *An Economic Theory of Democracy* (London: Harper and Row, 1957).
6. Institute of Economic Affairs, "The Economics of Politics," *Readings 18* (1978).
7. Richard Cockett, *Thinking the Unthinkable: Think Tanks and the Economic Counter Revolution, 1931–1983* (London: HarperCollins, 1994).
8. R. Kelf-Cohen, *Twenty Years of Nationalism: The British Experience* (London: Macmillan, 1969) and David Heald, "The Economic and

Financial Control of UK Nationalised Industries," *Economic Journal* vol. 90, no. 358 (June 1980).

9. Colin Robinson and Eileen Marshall, "Can Coal Be Saved?" *Hobart Paper 105*, Institute of Economic Affairs (1985).

10. Colin Robinson, "Energy Policy: Errors, Illusions and Market Realities," *Occasional Paper 90*, Institute of Economic Affairs, 1993.

11. Heald, op. cit.

12. M.E. Beesley and S.C. Littlechild, "Privatisation: Principles, Problems and Priorities," *Lloyds Bank Review* vol. 149 (July 1983).

13. W.L. Megginson, R.C. Nash, and M. van Randenborgh, "The Financial and Operating Performance of Newly Privatised Firms: An International Empirical Analysis," *Journal of Finance* vol. 49, no. 2 (1994).

14. Colin Robinson, "Profit, Discovery and the Role of Entry: The Case of Electricity," in *Regulating Utilities: A Time for Change? Readings 44*, Institute of Economic Affairs (1996).

15. Israel M. Kirzner, "How Markets Work: Disequilibrium, Entrepreneurship and Discovery," *Hobart Paper 133*, Institute of Economic Affairs, 1997.

16. Ibid. See also Israel M. Kirzner's "The Perils of Regulation: A Market Process Approach," in his *Discovery and the Capitalist Process* (Chicago, IL: University of Chicago Press, 1985).

17. Colin Robinson, "Freeing the Nuclear Industry," *Surrey Energy Economics Discussion Papers 85* (March 1996).

18. Robinson (1992) op. cit., Robinson (1993) op. cit., and Robinson "Introducing Competition into Water" in *Regulating Utilities: Broadening the Debate*, *Readings 46*, Institute of Economic Affairs (1997).

19. Robinson (1997), op. cit.

20. Ibid.

21. Colin Robinson, "Liberalising the Energy Industries," Proceedings of the Manchester Statistical Society, 1988.

22. Robinson (1997), op. cit.

23. H.A. Averch and L.L. Johnson, "Behavior of the Firm under Regulatory Constraint," *American Economic Review* vol. 52, no. 5 (December 1962).

24. Joseph Schumpeter, *Capitalism, Socialism and Democracy* (London: Allen and Unwin, 1976).

25. M.E. Beesley, "RPI-x: Principles and Their Application to Gas" in

Regulating Utilities: A Time for Change? Readings 44, Institute of Economic Affairs, 1996.

26. Robinson (1994), op. cit.

27. George J. Stigler, "The Theory of Economic Regulation," *Bell Journal of Economics and Management* vol. 2, no. 1 (Spring 1971) and Sam Pelzman, "Toward a More General Theory of Regulation," *Journal of Law and Economics* vol. 19, no. 2 (August 1976).

28. See Donald T. Brash, "New Zealand's Remarkable Reforms," *Occasional Paper 100*, Institute of Economic Affairs (1996), and A. Bollard and M. Pickford, "The New Zealand Solution: An Appraisal," in *Regulating Utilities: Broadening the Debate, Readings 46*, Institute of Economic Affairs (1997).

Notes on Chapter 8

1. Many recent works discuss the economic rationale behind privatization based on these and other objectives. See, for example, Energy Information Administration, "Privatization and the Globalization of Energy Markets," October 1996, 4; International Finance Corporation, "Privatization: Principles and Practice," 1995, 1; and Sunita Kikeri et al., "Privatization: the Lessons of Experience," The World Bank, 1992, 13–16. For a theoretical discussion, see Dieter Bos, *Privatization: A Theoretical Treatment* (Oxford: Clarendon Press, 1991), Chapter 1.

2. El Naggar notes that "the pattern of investment in the public sector is at variance with consideration of comparative advantage" (p. 2); and that "in many developing countries, there is evidence that the public sector is overextended and that privatization of a smaller or greater portion could produce only positive results in terms of improved efficiency, lower fiscal deficits, and better allocation of resources" (p. 3), in S. El-Naggar, *Privatization and Structural Adjustment* (Washington, DC: International Monetary Fund, 1989).

3. Bjorn Larson, "World Fossil Fuel Subsidies and Global Carbon Emissions in a Model with Interfuel Substitution," *Policy Research Working Paper No. 1256*, World Bank Policy Research Department, Washington, DC, 1994.

4. The detrimental effect on government budgets of tariffs that have been maintained well below the cost of supply are noted in Achilles G. Adamantiades et al. "Power Sector Reform in Developing Countries and the Role of the World Bank," Industry and Energy Department, *Occasional Paper No. 9*, September 1996. Also see Anil K. Malhotra and Ranjit Lamech, "Power Sector Experience in Asia," *Paper No. 8*, Asia Technical Department, The World Bank, Washington, DC, 1994.

5. John Nellis, "Is Privatization Necessary?" *Finance and Private Sector Development Department, Note 7*, The World Bank, Washington, DC, 1994. O. Chisari et al., "Winners and Losers from Utility Privatization in Argentina – Lessons from a General Equilibrium Model," *Policy Research Working Paper 1824*, Economic Development Institute, The World Bank, Washington, DC, 1997.

6. Bernard Tenenbaum et al., "Electricity Privatization: Structural, Competitive, and Regulatory Options," *Energy Policy* (UK) 20, December 1992, 1134–60.

7. Typical structures for private sector projects include build-own-operate (BOO) which allows the private owner to build, own, and operate the facility indefinitely; build-own-operate-transfer (BOOT) which implies that the concession for the operation will last a number of years, after which the assets are to revert to the government or its agency; and build-lease-transfer (BLT) which implies that the asset will be constructed by the investor who will lease (rather than own it) and then transferred back to the owner (the government or its agent) after a period of time. See Mangesh Hoskote, "Independent Power Projects (IPPs), An Overview," Finance and Private Sector Development Vice-Presidency, *Energy Note No. 2*, The World Bank, Washington, DC, 1995.

8. A. Mackie, "Electricity in the Middle East: Plugging the Power Gap," *Financial Times Energy Publications*, London, 1995.

9. The problem of subsidized electricity has been noted in many countries. For example, R. Stern noted in 1994 that prices to households in central and eastern Europe were still at around 50 percent of the economic cost level. See R. Stern, Presentation at the "Seminar on Regulation, Structure, and Pricing Decisions of Natural Monopolies III," Vienna, Austria, 23 August 1994.

10. O. Chisari et al., "Winners and Losers from Utility Privatization in Argentina – Lessons from a General Equilibrium Model," *Policy*

142 PRIVATIZATION AND DEREGULATION IN THE GULF ENERGY SECTOR

Research Working Paper 1824, Economic Development Institute, The World Bank, Washington, DC, September 1997.

11. "Limited recourse" financing means that the lenders have limited recourse to the assets of the parent company or project sponsors, up to project completion only; in "non-recourse" financing, lenders do not have recourse to the above assets at all. In both cases, lenders have recourse only to the project's assets and stream of revenues for repayment of the debt. This mode of financing is also known as "project financing" as opposed to "balance sheet financing."

Bibliography

Abu Shair, Osama J.A.R. *Privatization and Development* (New York: St Martin's Press, 1997).

Adam, Christopher. *Adjusting Privatization: Case Studies From Developing Countries* (London: J. Currey, 1992).

Adamantiades, Achilles G., John E. Besant-Jones, and Mangesh Hoskote. "Power Sector Reform in Developing Countries and the Role of the World Bank." Industry and Energy Department, *Occasional Paper No. 9*, September 1996. (Also presented at the 16th Congress of the World Energy Council, Tokyo, October 1995).

Adelman, M.A. *The Economics of Petroleum Supply: Papers by M.A. Adelman 1962–1993* (Cambridge, MA: MIT Press, 1993).

Aharoni, Yair. *Changing Roles of State Intervention in Services in an Era of Open International Markets* (Albany, NY: State University of New York Press, 1997).

Ahluwalia, S. S. "Financing energy investment in India – 1998 to 2012: The role of economic reform in bridging the demand-supply gap." Proceedings of the 20th International Conference of the International Association for Energy Economies, 1997.

Al-Mani, Saleh and Salah Al-Shaikhly. *The Euro-Arab Dialogue* (London: Frances Pinter, 1983).

Arab Banking Corporation. *The Arab Economies, 4th revised edition* (Bahrain: Arab Banking Corporation, 1994).

Arab Oil & Gas Directory (Paris: APRC, 1996).

Averch, H.A. and L.L. Johnson. "Behavior of the Firm under Regulatory Constraint." *American Economic Review* vol. 52, no. 5 (December 1962).

Ayres, Ian and John Braithwaite. *Responsive Regulation: Transcending the Deregulation Debate* (New York: Oxford University Press, 1992).

Azzam, Henry. *The Emerging Arab Capital Markets: Investment Opportunities in Relatively Underplayed Markets* (London: Kegan Paul International, 1997).

Bamberg, J.H. *The History of the British Petroleum Company vol. 2: The Anglo Iranian Years 1928–1954* (Cambridge: Cambridge University Press, 1994).

Banks, Eric. *Emerging Fixed-Income Markets in Asia: A Country-by-Country Guide to the Structure, Practices and Players of the World's Fastest Growing Debt Markets* (Chicago, IL: Probus, 1994).

Baumol, William J. and Gregory J. Sidak. *Transmission Pricing and Stranded Costs in the Electric Power Industry* (Washington, DC: AEI Press, 1995).

Beck, Robert J. *Worldwide Petroleum Industry Outlook, 1998–2002* (Tulsa, OK: Penn Well, 1997).

Beesley, M.E. and S.C. Littlechild. "Privatization: Principles, Problems and Priorities." *Lloyds Bank Review* vol. 149 (July 1983).

Bishop, M. et al. (eds) *Privatisation and Economic Performance* (Oxford: Oxford University Press, 1994).

Bos, Dieter. *Privatization: A Theoretical Treatment* (Oxford: Clarendon Press, 1991).

Boue, Juan Carlos. *Venezuela: The Political Economy of Oil* (Oxford: Oxford University Press, 1993).

BP (British Petroleum). *BP Statistical Review of World Energy 1997* (London: British Petroleum, 1997).

Brash, Donald T. "New Zealand's Remarkable Reforms." *Occasional Paper 100*, Institute of Economic Affairs (1996).

Butter, David. "Arabs seek common economic cause." *MEED*, 4 July 1997.

Calvo, Guillermo A. (ed.) *Private Capital Flows to Emerging Markets After the Mexican Crisis* (Washington, DC: Institute for International Economics, 1996).

Carter, Lawrence et al. *Investment Funds in Emerging Markets* (Washington, DC: World Bank, 1996).

Chaudhry, Kiren Aziz. *The Price of Wealth: Economics and Institutions in the Middle East* (Ithaca, NY: University of Cornell Press, 1997).

Chisari, O., A. Estache and C. Romero. "Winners and Losers from Utility Privatization in Argentina – Lessons from a General Equilibrium Model." *Policy Research Working Paper 1824*, Economic Development Institute (Washington, DC: World Bank, September 1997).

Claudon, M.P. and Tamar L. Gunter. *Comrades Go Private: Strategies for Eastern European Privatization* (New York: New York University Press, 1992).

Cockett, Richard. *Thinking the Unthinkable: Think Tanks and the Economic Counter Revolution, 1931–1983* (London: HarperCollins, 1994).

Cook, Paul and C.H. Kirkpatrick. *Privatization Policy and Performance: International Perspectives* (New York: Prentice Hall/Harvester Wheatsheaf, 1995).

Cowan, L.G. *Privatization in the Developing World* (New York: Greenwood Press, 1990).

Crystal, Jill. *Oil and Politics in the Gulf: Rulers Merchants in Kuwait and Qatar* (Cambridge: Cambridge University Press, 1995).

Dinavo, Jaques Vangu. *Privatization in Developing Countries: Its Impact on Economic Development and Democracy* (Westport, CT: Praeger, 1995).

Doran, Charles F. and Stephen W. Buck (eds) *The Gulf, Energy and Global Security: Political and Economic Issues* (Boulder, CO: Westview Press, 1991).

Downs, Anthony. *An Economic Theory of Democracy* (London: Harper and Row, 1957).

Duncan, Ian and Alan Bollard. *Corporatization and Privatization: Lessons from New Zealand* (Auckland: Oxford University Press, 1992).

Earle, John S. et al. *Privatization in the Transition to a Market Economy: Studies of Preconditions and Policies in Eastern Europe* (Prague: Central European University, 1993).

Ehteshami, Anoushiravan. "The Changing Balance of Power in Asia." *The Emirates Occasional Papers No. 16* (Abu Dhabi: ECSSR, 1998).

El Azhary, M.S. (ed.) *The Impact of Oil Revenues on Arab Gulf Development* (Boulder, CO: Westview Press, 1984).

El-Din, Hanaa Kheir. *Economic Cooperation in the Middle East: Prospects and Challenges* (Cairo: Dar Al-Mostaqbal Al-Arabia for Cairo University, Faculty of Economics and Political Science, 1995).

El-Naggar, S. *Privatization and Structural Adjustment* (Washington, DC: IMF, 1989).

Emery, James J. et al. *Technology Trade with the Middle East* (Boulder, CO: Westview Press, 1986).

Emirates Center for Strategic Studies and Research. *Gulf Energy and the World: Challenges and Threats* (London: I.B. Tauris, 1997).

— *Gulf Security in the Twenty-First Century* (London: I.B. Tauris, 1997).

— *Iran and the Gulf* (London: I.B. Tauris, 1996).

— *Strategic Positioning in the Oil Industry: Trends and Options* (London: I.B. Tauris, 1998).

— *The Information Revolution and the Arab World: Its Impact on State and Society* (London: I.B. Tauris, 1998).

Energy Information Administration. "Privatization and the Globalization of Energy Markets" (Washington, DC: US Department of Energy, 1996).

"Energy Impact of the Persian Gulf Crisis." Hearing before the Committee on Energy and Commerce, House of Representatives, One Hundred Second Congress, first session, 9 January 1991.

Fesharaki, Fereidun and David T. Isaak. *OPEC, the Gulf and the World Petroleum Market: A Study in Government Policy and Downstream Operations* (Boulder, CO: Westview Press, 1983).

Financial Times. *Electricity in the Middle East* (London: Financial Times Energy Publications, 1995).

Forsythe, Rosemarie. *The Politics of Oil in the Caucasus and Central Asia* (Oxford: Oxford University Press, 1996).

Galgoczi, Bela and Volkmar Kreissig. *Privatization, Enterprises, Participation: Case Studies in Eastern and Central Europe* (Munich: Mering, R. Hampp, 1995).

Gavin, L. "Gulf Funds primed for privatization." *MEED*, 13 June 1997.

Gayle, Dennis J. and Jonathan N. Goodrich. *Privatization and Deregulation in Global Perspective* (Westport, CT: Quorum Books, 1990).

GCC Business and Finance Guide 1996/97 (Bahrain: Gulf Investment Corporation and Gulf International Bank, 1997).

George, Robert Lloyd and Sal Randazzo. *The Handbook of Emerging Markets: A Country-by-Country Guide to the World's Fastest Growing Economies* (Chicago, IL: Probus, 1995).

Ghantus, Elias T. *Arab Economic Integration* (London: Croom Helm, 1982).

Glade, William and Rossana Corona. *Bigger Economies, Smaller Governments: Privatization in Latin America* (Boulder, CO: Westview Press, 1996).

Glen, Jack. *An Introduction to the Microstructure of Emerging Markets* (Washington, DC: World Bank, 1994).

Glen, Jack D. and Yannis Karmokolias. *Dividend Policy and Behavior in Emerging Markets: To Pay or Not to Pay* (Washington, DC: World Bank, 1995).

Gordon, R.L., H.D. Jacoby, and M.B. Zimmerman (eds) *Energy: Markets and Regulation* (Cambridge, MA: MIT Press, 1987).

Gormley, William T. *Privatization and Its Alternatives* (Madison, WI: University of Wisconsin Press, 1991).

Government of India. *Economic Survey* (various issues) (New Delhi: Ministry of Finance, Government of India).

— *Indian Petroleum and Natural Gas Statistics* 1996/97 (New Delhi: Economics and Statistics Division, Ministry of Petroleum and Natural Gas).

Guazzone, Laura (ed.) *The Middle East in Global Change: The Politics and Economics of Interdependence Versus Fragmentation* (New York: St Martin's Press, 1997).

Guislain, Pierre. *The Privatisation Challenge* (Washington, DC: The World Bank, 1997).

Hanke, H. (ed.) *Privatization and Development* (San Francisco, CA: International Center for Economic Growth, ICS Press, 1987).

Harik, Iliya F. and Denis J. Sullivan. *Privatization and Liberalization in the Middle East* (Bloomington, IN: Indiana University Press, 1992).

Harrison, J. and A. Gretton (eds) *Energy UK 1986* (London: Newbury, 1986).

Harthshorn, J.E. *Oil Trade: Politics and Prospects* (Cambridge: Cambridge University Press, 1993).

Hawdon, D. (ed.) *The Changing Structure of the World Oil Industry* (London: Croom Helm, 1984).

Heald, David. "The Economic and Financial Control of UK Nationalized Industries." *Economic Journal* vol. 90, no. 358 (June 1980).

Hines, Mary A. *The Development and Finance of Global Private Power* (Westport, CT: Quorum Books, 1997).

Hoopes, Stephanie M. *Oil Privatization, Public Choice and International Forces* (New York: St Martin's Press, 1997).

Hopfinger, Hans. *Economic Liberalization and Privatization in Socialist Arab Countries: Algeria, Egypt, Syria and Yemen* (Gotha: Justus Perthes Verlag Gotha, 1996).

Horsnell, Paul. *Oil in Asia: Markets, Trading, Refining and Deregulation* (Oxford: Oxford University Press for the Oxford Institute for Energy Studies, 1997).

Hoskote, Mangesh. "Independent Power Projects (IPPs), An Overview." Finance and Private Sector Development Vice-Presidency, *Energy Note No. 2* (Washington, DC: World Bank, May 1995).

Hutton, W. *The State We Are In* (London: Jonathan Cape, 1993).

Institute of Economic Affairs. "The Economics of Politics" *Readings 18* (1978).

— "Regulating Utilities: A Time for Change?" *Readings 44* (1996).

— "Regulating Utilities: Broadening the Debate." *Readings 46* (1997).

International Finance Corporation. *Privatization: Principles and Practice* (Washington, DC: IFC, 1995).

Iskandar, S. "Privatization: Mixed signals sent over sell-offs." *Financial Times*, 22 September 1997.

Issawi, Charles Philip. *The Economies of Middle Eastern Oil* (New York: Praeger, 1962).

Jackson, Peter and Catherine Price. *Privatization and Regulation: A Review of the Issues* (London: Longman, 1994).

Jacobson, David and Bernadette Andreosso-O'Callaghan. *Industrial Economics and Organization: A European Perspective* (London: McGraw-Hill, 1996).

Kapoor, Ashok. *International Business in the Middle East: Case Studies* (Boulder, CO: Westview Press, 1979).

Kay, J.A. et al. *Privatization and Regulation: The UK Experience* (New York: Oxford University Press, 1996).

Kelf-Cohen, R. *Twenty Years of Nationalism: The British Experience* (London: Macmillan, 1969).

Keppler, Michael and Martin Lechner. *Emerging Markets: Research, Strategies and Benchmarks* (New York: Irwin Professional Publications 1996).

Kikeri, Sunita et al. *Privatization: The Lessons of Experience* (Washington, DC: World Bank, 1992).

Kirzner, Israel M. *Discovery and the Capitalist Process* (Chicago, IL: University of Chicago Press, 1985).

— "How Markets Work: Disequilibrium, Entrepreneurship and Discovery." *Hobart Paper 133*, Institute of Economic Affairs (1997).

Kramer, Ralph M. *Privatization in Four European Countries: Comparative Studies in Government-Third Sector Relationships* (Armonk, NY: M.E. Sharpe, 1993).

Kubursi, Atif A. and Thomas Naylor (eds). *Co-operation and Development in the Energy Sector: The Arab Gulf States and Canada* (Dover, NH: Croom Helm, 1985).

Kumar, P.C. *Internal Sources of Development Finance: Concepts, Issues and Strategies* (Westport, CT: Quorum Books, 1994).

Laffont, Jean-Jacques and Jean Tirole. *A Theory of Incentives in Procurement and Regulation* (Cambridge, MA: MIT Press, 1993).

Larsen, Bjorn. "World Fossil Fuel Subsidies and Global Carbon Emissions in a Model with Interfuel Substitution." *Policy Research Working Paper No. 1256* (Washington, DC: World Bank, 1994).

Letta, Corrado. *Listening to the Emerging Markets of Southeast Asia: Long Term Strategies for Effective Partnerships* (New York: J. Wiley, 1996).

Levy, Sidney. *Build, Operate, Transfer: Paving the Way for Tomorrow's Infra-structure* (New York: J. Wiley, 1996).

Lieberman, Ira W. *Privatization and Emerging Equity Markets* (Washington, DC: World Bank, 1998).

Longhurst, Henry. *Adventure in Oil: The Story of British Petroleum* (London: Sidgwick and Jackson, 1959).

Lucas, Robert E. Jr. "Economic Policy Evaluation: A Critique," Carnegie Rochester Conference Series on Public Policy, no. 1, 1976.

— *Studies in Business-Cycle Theory* (Cambridge, MA: MIT Press, 1981).

Mabro, Robert, Robert Bacon, Margaret Chadwick, Mark Halliwell, and David Long. *The Market for North Sea Crude Oil* (Oxford: Oxford University Press, 1986).

MacAvoy, Paul W. *Energy Policy: An Economic Analysis* (New York: Norton, 1983).

MacKerron, G. and P. Pearson (eds) *The UK Energy Experience: A Model or Warning?* (London: Imperial College Press, 1996).

Mackie, A. *Electricity in the Middle East: Plugging the Power Gap* (London: Financial Times Energy Publications, 1995).

Malhotra, Anil K. and Ranjit Lamech. "Power Sector Experience in Asia." *Paper No. 8*, Asia Technical Department (Washington, DC: World Bank, 1994).

Maloney, W.A. *Managing Policy Change in Britain: The Politics of Water* (Edinburgh: Edinburgh University Press, 1995).

Martin, Stephen and David Parker. *The Impact of Privatization: Ownership and Corporate Performance in the UK* (New York: Routledge, 1997).

Megginson, W.L., R.C. Nash, and M. van Randenborgh. "The Financial and Operating Performance of Newly Privatized Firms: An International Empirical Analysis." *Journal of Finance* vol. 49, no. 2 (1994).

Michalet, C.A. *Rebalancing the Public and Private Sectors: Developing Country Experience* (Paris: OECD Development Centre, 1991)

Milor, Vedat. *Changing Political Economies: Privatization in Post-communist and Reforming Communist States* (Boulder, CO: Lynne Rienner Publishers, 1994).

Ministerio de Economia y Obras y Servicios Publicos. *Argentina's Privatization Programme: Gas, Energy, Maritime Transport, Mailing, Saving Bank and Insurance* (Buenos Aires: Ministry of Economy and Public Works and Services, 1992).

Mitchell, J.V. et al. *The New Geopolitics of Energy* (London: RIIA, 1996).

Mobius, Mark. *The Investor's Guide to Emerging Markets* (New York: Irwin Professional Publications, 1994).

Morgan, Philip I. *Privatization and the Welfare State: Implications for Consumers and the Workforce* (Brookfield, VT: Dartmouth Publishing Company, 1995).

Munasinghe, Mohan. *Electric Power Economics* (London: Butterworths, 1990).

Naser, Kamal. "Investment Prospects in a Sample of Arab Stock Exchanges." *The Emirates Occasional Papers No. 17* (Abu Dhabi: ECSSR, 1998).

Naser, Kamal and Y. Younis. "Privatization moves to the heavy industry." *MEED*, 23 May 1997.

Naya, Seiji. *Private Sector Development and Enterprise Reforms in Growing Asian Economies* (San Francisco, CA: ICS Press, 1990).

Nellis, John. "Is Privatization Necessary?" *Finance and Private Sector Development Department Note 7* (Washington, DC: World Bank, 1994).

Niblock, Tim and Emma Murphy. *Economic and Political Liberalization in the Middle East* (New York: British Academic Press, 1993)

OECD. *Privatization in Asia, Europe and Latin America* (Paris: OECD, 1996).

— "Privatization: Recent Trends." *Financial Market Trends 66* (March 1997).

— "Recent Trends in Privatization." *Financial Market Trends 64* (June 1996).

— *Methods of Privatizing Large Enterprises* (Paris: OECD, 1993).

— *Middle East Oil and Gas* (Paris: OECD/IEA, 1995).

— *Private Sector Development: A Guide to Donor Support* (Paris: OECD, 1995).

Pakravan, Karim. *Oil Supply Disruptions in the 1980s: An Economic Analysis* (Stanford, CA: Hoover Press, 1984).

Park, Keith K.H. and Antoine W. Van Agtmael (eds) *The World's Emerging Stock Markets: Structure, Developments, Regulations and Opportunities* (Chicago, IL: Probus, 1993).

Parker, David. *Privatization in the European Union: Theory and Policy Perspectives* (New York: Routledge, 1998).

Peacock, A.T. "Privatization in Perspective." *Three Banks Review* vol. 144 (December 1984).

Pelkmans, Jacques, and Norbert Wagner. *Privatization and Deregulation in ASEAN and the EC: Making Markets More Effective* (Singapore: Institute of Southeast Asian Studies, 1990).

Pelzman, Sam. "Toward a More General Theory of Regulation." *Journal of Law and Economics* vol. 19, no. 2 (August 1976).

Pirie, Madsen. *Privatization* (Aldershot: Hampshire, Wildwood House, 1988).

Ramanadham, V.V. *Constraints and Impacts of Privatization* (London: Routledge, 1993).

— *Privatization and Equity* (London: Routledge, 1995).

Richards, Alan and John Waterbury. *A Political Economy of the Middle East* (Boulder, CO: Westview Press, 1996).

Robins, Philip. *The Future of the Gulf: Politics and Oil in the 1990s* (Brookfield, VT: Gower Publications, 1989).

Robinson, Colin. "Energy Policy: Errors, Illusions and Market Realities." *Occasional Paper 90*, Institute of Economic Affairs (1993).

— "Freeing the Nuclear Industry." *Surrey Energy Economics Discussion Papers 85* (March 1996).

— "Gas After the MMC Verdict" in *Regulating Utilities: The Way Forward, Readings 41*, Institute of Economic Affairs (1994).

— "Liberalizing the Energy Industries." Proceedings of the Manchester Statistical Society (1988).

— "Privatizing the Energy Industries: The Lessons to be Learned." *Metreoeconomica* vol. 43, nos. 1–2 (February–June 1992).

Robinson, Colin and Eileen Marshall. "Can Coal be Saved?" *Hobart Paper 105*, Institute of Economic Affairs (1985).

Rodinelli, Dennis A. *Privatization and Economic Reform in Central Europe: The Changing Business Climate* (Westport, CT: Quorum, 1994).

Roth, Gabriel J. *The Private Provision of Public Services in Developing Countries* (New York: Oxford University Press, 1987).

Roukis, George S. and Patrick J. Montana (eds) *Workforce Management in the Arabian Peninsula: Forces Affecting Development* (Westport, CT: Greenwood Press, 1986).

Salamon, L. M. and Michael S. Lund. *Beyond Privatization: The Tools of Government Action* (Washington, DC: Urban Institute Press, 1989)

Sassanpour, Cyrus. *Policy Challenges in the Gulf Cooperation Council Countries* (Washington, DC: Middle Eastern Department, IMF, 1996).

Schumpeter, Joseph. *Capitalism, Socialism and Democracy* (London: Allen and Unwin, 5th Edition, 1976).

Shaikh, Abdul Hafeez. *The Rise, Decline and Future of Public Enterprises* (Boston, MA: Harvard University, 1991).

— *Argentina Privatization Program: A Review of Five Cases* (Washington, DC: The World Bank, 1997).

Shaker, Sallama. *State, Society and Privatization in Turkey, 1979–1990* (Washington, DC: Woodrow Wilson Center Press, 1995).

Sharma, Shankar (ed.) *Energy, Environment and the Oil Market: An Asia-Pacific Perspective* (Singapore: Institute of Southeast Asian Studies, 1995).

Sick, Gary and Lawrence Potter (eds). *The Persian Gulf at the Millennium: Essays in Politics, Economy, Security and Religion* (New York: St Martin's Press, 1998).

Singh, A. "Corporate Financial Patterns in Industrializing Economies." *IFC Technical Paper No. 2* (Washington, DC: IFC, 1995).

Smith, Graham (ed.) *Getting Connected: Private Participation in Infrastructure in the Middle East and North Africa* (Washington, DC: World Bank, 1997).

Spulber, Nicolas. *Economics of Water Resources: From Regulation to Privatization* (Boston, MA: Kluwer Academic, 1998).

Stigler, George J. "The Theory of Economic Regulation." *Bell Journal of Economics and Management* vol. 2, no. 1 (Spring 1971).

Surrey, J. (ed.) *The British Electricity Experiment* (London: Earthscan, 1996)

Swann, Dennis. *The Retreat of the State: Deregulation and Privatization in the UK and US* (New York: Harvester Wheatsheaf, 1988).

Syu, Agnes. *From Economic Miracle to Privatization Success: Initial Stages of the Privatization Process in Two SOEs on Taiwan* (Lanham, MD: University Press of America, 1995).

Tanyi, Gerald Bisong. *Designing Privatization Strategies in Africa: Law, Economics and Practice* (Westport, CT: Praeger, 1997).

Tata Energy Research Institute. *TERI Energy Data Directory and Yearbook 1990* (New Delhi: Tata Energy Research Institute, 1990).

— *TERI Energy Data Directory and Yearbook 1997/98* (New Delhi: Tata Energy Research Institute, 1997).

Tenenbaum, Bernard, Reinier Lock, and James V. Barker. "Electricity Privatization: Structural, Competitive, and Regulatory Options." *Energy Policy* 20 (December 1992).

Teplitz-Sembitzky, W. *Regulation or Deregulation – What is Needed in the LDSs Power Sector* (Washington, DC: World Bank, 1990).

Tye, W.B. and John R. Meyer. *The Transition to Deregulation: Developing Economic Standards for Public Policies* (New York: Quorum Books, 1991).

United Nations Economic Commission for Western Asia. *Economic Integration in Western Asia* (London: Frances Pinter, 1985).

Veljanovski, C.G. *Privatization and Competition: A Market Prospectus* (London: Institute of Economic Affairs, 1999).

Vickers, John and George Yarrow. *Privatization: An Economic Analysis* (Cambridge, MA: MIT Press, 1988).

— *Privatization and the Natural Monopolies* (London: Public Policy Centre, 1985).

Vogel, Steven K. *Freer Markets, More Rules: Regulatory Reform in Advanced Industrial Countries* (Ithaca, NY: Cornell University Press, 1996).

Walker, John S. *A Financial-agency Analysis of Privatization: Managerial Incentives and Financial Contracting* (Bethlehem, PA: Leigh University Press, 1997).

Weidenfeld, Werner. *Europe and the Middle East* (Gütersloh: Bertelsmann Foundation, 1995).

Welch, Dick and Olivier Fremond. "The Case-by-Case Approach to Privatization: Techniques and Examples." *World Bank Technical Paper No. 403* (Washington, DC: World Bank, 1998).

Weyman-Jones, T.G. *Electricity Privatization* (Brookfield, VT: Averbury, 1989).

Whynes, David K. and Roger A. Bowles. *The Economic Theory of the State* (Oxford: Martin Robertson, 1981).

Wilson, Rodney. "The Changing Composition and Direction of GCC Trade." *The Emirates Occasional Papers No. 18* (Abu Dhabi: ECSSR, 1998).

— *Economic Development in the Middle East* (London: Routledge, 1987).

— *Islamic Finance* (London: Financial Times Publications, 1997).

— *Economic Development in the Middle East* (London: Routledge, 1995).

— *Euro-Arab Trade*. Economist Intelligence Unit, Report 1105 (London: The Economist, 1988).

World Bank. *World Development Report* (Washington, DC: World Bank, 1993).

— *The State in a Changing World* (Washington, DC: World Bank, 1997).

— *World Development Indicators* (Washington, DC: World Bank, 1997).

World Trade Organization Annual Report (Geneva: World Trade Organization, 1996).

Wright, Vincent. *Privatization in Western Europe: Pressures, Problems and Paradoxes* (New York: Frances Pinter, 1994).

Yarrow, George K. and Piotr Jasinski. *Privatization: Critical Perspectives on the World Economy* (London: Routledge, 1996).

Yergin, Daniel. *The Prize* (New York: Simon & Schuster, 1991).

— *The Commanding Heights: The Battle Between Government and the Marketplace that is Remaking the Modern World* (New York: Simon & Schuster, 1998).

Zahariadis, Nikolaos. *Markets, States and Public Policy: Privatization in Britain and France* (Ann Arbor, MI: The University of Michigan Press, 1995).

Index